CELEBRATING THE HOLY EUCHARIST

FRANCIS CARDINAL ARINZE

CELEBRATING THE HOLY EUCHARIST

IGNATIUS PRESS   SAN FRANCISCO

Cover art: *The Last Supper* (detail)
Ste. Chapelle, Paris
© Art Resource, New York

Cover design by Roxanne Mei Lum

© 2006 Ignatius Press, San Francisco

ISBN 978-1-58617-158-2 (HB)
ISBN 1-58617-158-5 (HB)
Library of Congress Control Number 2006921885
Printed in the United States of America ∞

CONTENTS

PREFACE

The Eucharistic celebration occupies a central place in the prayer life of the Church and, therefore, of every member of the Church. The Church herself takes her origin from the paschal mystery of the suffering, death, and Resurrection of Christ. When she celebrates this mystery in the Holy Eucharist, she is at the high point of her public worship. She also finds herself, in the Eucharistic celebration, at the fount from which all her power flows.

The priest is ordained in the first place to celebrate the Sacrifice of the Mass and then to carry out other liturgical rites, to preach the Word of God, and to gather the people of God together. He is at the summit of his vocation when *in persona Christi* he celebrates the Eucharistic Sacrifice.

The lay faithful and men and women of the consecrated life in its many forms find in the Eucharistic celebration the fount and apex of their entire Christian lives and the spiritual powerhouse from which their apostolates are given life, meaning, and a sense of direction.

I have therefore accepted the request of several friends to prepare the following reflections on the celebration of the Eucharistic mystery. Most of these meditations have been proposed to various congregations in seminars, congresses, or homilies in the past three years. In view of the Year of the Eucharist that was concluded in October 2005 with the XI Ordinary Assembly of the Synod of Bishops, the theme seems of particular relevance. But even independently of this

Year of the Eucharist, the celebration of the Eucharistic mystery remains of prime importance in our lives as followers of Christ. In a sense, we can never say enough about the Holy Eucharist.

Without, therefore, pretending to say anything entirely new, I offer the following reflections for the use of priests, deacons, men and women of the consecrated life, and the lay faithful. I hope that these theological, pastoral, and liturgical considerations may help improve the quality of their various contributions to the celebration of the Holy Mass and their veneration of the Holy Eucharist outside Mass.

This book begins with a reflection on the Holy Eucharist as sacrifice and sacrament, on the importance of faith on our part, and on the necessity of reverence due to our Blessed Lord in this mystery. Reverence also calls for some periods of silence and contemplation during the Eucharistic celebration.

Every Christian has a role in the celebration. Thoughts are directed to the roles of the diocesan Bishop, the celebrating priest, and the liturgical assembly in general. The active participation of all the baptized will be examined together with its necessary bodily dimension. Temptations to exaggerate will also be mentioned.

Not a few changes have been introduced in liturgical rites especially in the past forty years. A general look at them with reference to the Mass will be useful. Here we will consider the place of adaptation and inculturation with regard to Mass and the importance of observing established liturgical norms.

The Eucharistic celebration sends Christians on mission, to evangelize. Deserving of special mention is the role of the family, apart from that of individuals, in this evangelizing mission.

The veneration of the Holy Eucharist outside Mass has

found many expressions in the life of the Church, especially of the Latin Rite. It should therefore be discussed.

In order to appreciate fully and to live out the centrality of the Eucharist in their faith, all Christians need ongoing scriptural and liturgical formation.

These reflections, prepared in August 2005, have been enriched with insights from the XI Assembly of the Synod of Bishops, which met in the Vatican City in October 2005.

May our Blessed Mother Mary, "Woman of the Eucharist" (EE 53), obtain for us the grace to grow in our Eucharistic faith and in ever deeper sharing in the Eucharistic celebration.

Vatican City
Solemnity of Christ the King, 2005

WHAT THE CHURCH TEACHES
ON THE HOLY EUCHARIST

The Holy Eucharist, says the Second Vatican Council, "contains the Church's entire spiritual wealth: Christ himself, our passover and living bread" (PO 5; see also EE 1). In considering, therefore, the celebration of this spiritual treasure, it is fitting that we begin with a listing of Gospel and other New Testament passages along with some major documents of the Magisterium on the Holy Eucharist.

New Testament and Magisterial Documents

In the Gospel according to John, chapter 6, Jesus promises us the Holy Eucharist and teaches us its key place. Three accounts of the institution are to be found in Matthew 26:26–29; Mark 14:12–16, 22–26; and Luke 22:19–20; and another in 1 Corinthians 11:23–26.

The major liturgical books on the Eucharistic celebration are the *Roman Missal*, third typical edition of 2002 (with 1,318 pages!), and the lectionary.

The major corpus of teaching of the Catholic faith regarding the Holy Eucharist by an ecumenical or general council is that of the Council of Trent (1545–1563), especially as recorded in DS 1725–60. The Second Vatican Council (1962–1965) also gave precious considerations, teaching, and directives on the Holy Eucharist and its celebration in *Lumen Gentium* and *Sacrosanctum Concilium*.

The *Catechism of the Catholic Church*, as an up-to-date compendium of what the Church believes and teaches, supported by papal authority, will be found to be a special guide, especially in articles 1322 to 1405.

Among papal documents in the last sixty years, allow me to mention the three Encyclical Letters *Mediator Dei* by Pius XII in 1947, *Mysterium Fidei* by Paul VI in 1965, and *Ecclesia de Eucharistia* by John Paul II in 2003. Three Apostolic Letters of the last-named Pope are also on the Holy Eucharist: *Dominicae Cenae* in 1980, *Dies Domini* in 1998, and *Mane Nobiscum Domine* in 2004.

It is also useful to study the five following documents of the Congregation for Divine Worship and the Discipline of the Sacraments: *Eucharisticum Mysterium* in 1967, *Eucharistiae Sacramentum* in 1973, *Directory on Popular Devotion and Liturgy* in 2002, *Redemptionis Sacramentum* in 2004, and *Suggestions and Proposals for the Year of the Eucharist* in 2004.

Holy Eucharist: Sacrifice: Memorial of Our Redemption

At the Last Supper, the night before he gave his life for us on the Cross, our Lord Jesus Christ took bread, gave thanks, and said to his Apostles: "This is my Body given for you." He did the same with the cup after supper and said: "This cup is the new covenant in my blood poured out for you" (Lk 22:9–20). Jesus gave to his Apostles his Body to eat and his Blood to drink. Then he added: "Whenever you drink it, do this as a memorial of me" (1 Cor 11:25). And Saint Paul explains to the Corinthians: "Whenever you eat this bread, then, and drink this cup, you are proclaiming the Lord's death until he comes" (1 Cor 11:26).

The Eucharistic celebration is the sacramental re-presentation of the paschal mystery, that is, of the suffering, death, and Resurrection of Christ. When the Church celebrates the Eucharist, she celebrates the memorial of Christ's Passover, or Easter, Mystery, which becomes present. The sacrifice that Christ offered once and for all on the Cross becomes actually present. "As often as the sacrifice of the Cross by which 'Christ our Pasch has been sacrificed' is celebrated on the altar, the work of our redemption is carried out" (LG 3; cf. CCC 1364 and 1 Cor 5:7).

Jesus our Savior was already symbolized as victim in Isaac and the paschal lamb and as food in the manna given to the chosen people during their forty years in the desert. It is this Jesus who gives himself to us in the Holy Eucharist every day of our earthly pilgrimage, until we reach the promised land of heaven. Saint Thomas Aquinas rightly sings in the *Lauda Sion Salvatorem*:

> Christ willed what he himself had done
> Should be renewed while time should run,
> In memory of his parting hour;
> Thus, tutored in his school divine,
> We consecrate the bread and wine;
> And lo—a Host of saving power. . . .
>
> Oft in olden types foreshadowed;
> In Isaac on the altar bowed,
> And in the ancient paschal food,
> And in the manna sent from heaven.

That the Holy Eucharist is a sacrifice is already manifested in the very words of Christ, who gave us this mystery: "This is my Body given for you", and "This cup is the new covenant in my Blood poured out for you" (Lk 22:19–20). At Holy Mass Christ gives the same Body that he handed over for us on the Cross and the same Blood "of the covenant, poured out for many for the forgiveness of sins" (Mt 26:28; cf. CCC 1365).

Therefore this memorial of our redemption, the Eucharistic Sacrifice, or the Mass, is one and the same sacrifice as the sacrifice of the Cross on Mount Calvary. "The victim is one and the same: the same now offers through the ministry of priests, who then offered himself on the Cross; only the manner of offering is different" (Council of Trent: DS 1743; cf. CCC 1367).

When, therefore, the Lord Jesus gathers us around the altar for Holy Mass, we are like those disciples who stood at the foot of the Cross on Mount Calvary, together with the Most Blessed Virgin Mary.

Why Offer Holy Mass?

It is important that we be convinced why the Eucharistic Sacrifice is necessary. Indeed, it is the virtue of religion at its heart and its highest point.

God created us. He preserves us in existence. In him we live and move and exist (see Acts 17:28). His Providence governs all that he has created. He takes individual care of each of us and knows us by name (see Is 49:1). As his creatures who have intelligence and will, we owe him adoration, praise, and thanksgiving. Because we are sinners, some more than others, we should turn to him with acts of repentance and propitiation. And because everything we need, spiritual and temporal, comes from him, we make prayers of petition.

Whoever does all that is practicing the virtue of religion.

And the Sacrifice of the Mass is offered precisely for those reasons: adoration and praise, thanksgiving, propitiation, and supplication, in that order of priority. The Eucharistic Sacrifice is therefore at the very heart of the virtue of religion.

It is important to appreciate the vertical dimension of the Mass. This act of worship is primarily directed toward God to adore him, praise him, and thank him. God is supreme, transcendent, and great above all we can ever imagine. We owe him the loving tribute of adoration. Through the Eucharistic Sacrifice we also praise and thank God for his work of creation, for having loved us so much that he sent his only begotten Son for our salvation, and for sanctifying us through his Holy Spirit (cf. CCC 1359–61).

We are sinners. God is holy, three times holy, holiness itself (see Is 6:3). By sin we offend God. Only Jesus Christ, the Son of God made man, could adequately make amends to God's infinite majesty for original sin and for our personal offenses. And he is the Victim who offers himself to the Eternal Father in the Eucharistic Sacrifice and associates his Church with himself in this supreme act of worship.

It is necessary to underline this vertical dimension, this God-ward direction of the Mass, because of the ever present temptation to horizontalism. People often come to Mass because they have needs to present before God. This is not wrong. But priority goes to adoration, praise, thanksgiving, and propitiation, not to ourselves and what we need. It is even more mistaken if people come to Mass in order to enjoy the music, to admire the preacher, to show off their talents, or to engage in mutual admiration and affirmation between priest and people. If we are to allow the Holy Eucharist to exert its great power in our Christian vocation and mission, we have to learn to see it first as primarily an act of worship directed toward God.

Holy Eucharist: Sacrament: Real Presence

In the most Holy Eucharist, Jesus Christ is really present. He remains with us. His words are clear. They are not equivocal. They are not ambiguous: "This is my Body. . . . This is my Blood." The way in which Christ is present in this sacrament is unique. It raises the Holy Eucharist above all the other sacraments and makes it "the perfection of the spiritual life and the end to which all the sacraments tend".[1]

As the Council of Trent teaches us, in the Most Blessed Sacrament of the Eucharist "the body and blood, together with the soul and divinity, of our Lord Jesus Christ and, therefore, *the whole Christ is truly, really, and substantially* contained" (DS 1651; see CCC 1374).

We should carefully distinguish between the real presence of Christ in the Holy Eucharist and his other forms of presence. Of course Jesus is present in liturgical celebrations, in the person of the priest who is his minister, in the ministers of the other sacraments, in the Word of God proclaimed, and in the liturgical assembly of the faithful (see SC 7). But the presence of Christ in the Most Holy Eucharist surpasses all these other types of presence. It is therefore rightly called the Real Presence, not because the other forms of presence are not real, too, "but because it is presence in the fullest sense: that is to say, it is a *substantial* presence by which Christ, God and man, makes himself wholly and entirely present" (MF 39).

The Council of Trent summarizes the Catholic faith by declaring:

Because Christ our Redeemer said that it was truly his body that he was offering under the species of bread, it has always

---

[1] Saint Thomas Aquinas, ST III, 73, 3c.

been the conviction of the Church of God, and this holy Council now declares again, that by the consecration of the bread and wine there takes place a change of the whole substance of the bread into the substance of the body of Christ our Lord and of the whole substance of the wine into the substance of his blood. This change the holy Catholic Church has fittingly and properly called transubstantiation. (DS 1642; see CCC 1376)

It is with the whole tradition of the Church that we believe that under the appearances of bread and wine, Jesus is really present. "Faith demands that we approach the Eucharist fully aware that we are approaching Christ himself. . . . The Eucharist is a mystery of presence, the perfect fulfillment of Jesus' promise to remain with us until the end of the world" (MND 16).

The Holy Eucharist Nourishes Us

Jesus nourishes us in the sacrament of the Holy Eucharist. We absolutely need him in order to have life. His teaching is clear and unmistakable. "If you do not eat the flesh of the Son of Man and drink his blood, you have no life in you" (Jn 6:53). In case this is still not clear to anyone, he continues: "For my flesh is real food and my blood is real drink" (Jn 6:55).

Jesus promises a wonderful and hitherto unheard-of union between himself and the disciple who receives him in this sacrament: "As the living Father sent me and I draw life from the Father, so whoever eats me will also draw life from me" (Jn 6:57). Is this not an exceptionally precious assurance from our Blessed Lord and Savior? When we receive Jesus in this sacrament, we abide in him and he in us. This is of crucial importance if we want to produce lasting fruit in the apostolate, in our mission for Christ. He himself told the

Apostles at the Last Supper: "Remain in me, as I in you. As a branch cannot bear fruit all by itself, unless it remains part of the vine, neither can you unless you remain in me" (Jn 15:4).

By our communion in the Body and Blood of Christ, we also receive an increase of the gift of the Holy Spirit, who was already poured into us at Baptism and bestowed as a seal in Confirmation (cf. EE 17). In the third Eucharistic Prayer, the Church confesses this: "Grant that we who are nourished by his Body and Blood may be filled with his Holy Spirit, and become one body, one spirit in Christ."

Holy Eucharist: Bread for Our Journey

When the people of Israel whom Moses had led through the Red Sea were in the desert, they were hungry and thirsty. They complained against Moses and Aaron: "You have led us into this desert to starve this entire assembly to death." And their complaints were not in vain. Moses appealed to God. God sent that large assembly manna from heaven to eat. And this lasted for forty years until they entered the promised land (see Ex 16).

The manna was a symbol of the Holy Eucharist. The teaching of Jesus at Capernaum is clear: "I am the bread of life. Your fathers ate manna in the desert and they are dead; but this is the bread which comes down from heaven, so that a person may eat it and not die. I am the living bread which has come down from heaven. Anyone who eats this bread will live for ever; and the bread that I shall give is my flesh for the life of the world" (Jn 6:48–51).

The Holy Eucharist is the bread for our earthly pilgrimage symbolized by the forty years spent by the chosen people in the desert. When people prepare themselves well and receive Jesus in Holy Communion, he produces in them wonderful fruits. This sacrament augments our union with Christ. It is Jesus himself who gives us this guarantee: "Whoever eats my flesh and drinks my blood lives in me, and I live in him" (Jn 6:56).

Holy Communion separates us from sin, cleanses us from sin, and preserves us from future sins by strengthening us against temptation and increasing our taste for the things of God. As bodily nourishment restores lost strength, so the Holy Eucharist strengthens our charity (see CCC 1392–95).

The Holy Eucharist prepares us for entry into eternal glory. It guides and strengthens us in our earthly exile as we "await the blessed hope and the coming of our Savior, Jesus Christ" (RM, embolism after the *Pater Noster*). Jesus himself promised: "Anyone who eats this bread will live for ever" (Jn 6:51, 58).

Holy Eucharist: Sacrament of Unity

In 1 Corinthians 10:16–17, Saint Paul stresses the Holy Eucharist as a sacrament of unity, a bond of charity. We all drink from the one chalice of the Blood of Christ. One loaf, one body: so are all of us who receive the same Jesus Christ in this most Blessed Sacrament.

Since all those who, well prepared, receive Holy Communion become more closely united with Christ, they by that fact also become more closely united in the one body that is the Church. The Holy Eucharist renews, strengthens, and deepens this incorporation into the Church that began already in Baptism. Saint Augustine puts it this way: "You hear the words, 'the Body of Christ' and respond 'Amen.' Be then a member of the Body of Christ that your *Amen* may be true." [2]

---

[2] Saint Augustine, *Sermo* 272 (PL 38, 1247); see also CCC 1396.

The Church therefore prays over the offerings at the Votive Mass of the Holy Eucharist that this sacrament of love may be for us the sign of unity and the bond of charity. And in the Prayer after Communion the Church prays that by the Body and Blood of Christ, God may join all his people in brotherly love.

This shows us how important it is that we love one another and that, if we have some quarrel or disagreement with our neighbor, we should do our best to be reconciled. Only then will our Eucharistic celebration and Communion be allowed to bring us maximum fruit. This is the unambiguous teaching of our Lord: "If you are bringing your offering to the altar and there remember that your brother has something against you, leave your offering there before the altar, go and be reconciled with your brother first, and then come back and present your offering" (Mt 5:23–24).

Holy Communion: Adequate Preparation

The wonderful effects of Holy Communion are not automatic. They demand from the communicant adequate preparation. The most important form of preparation is that the person be in a state of grace. It would be a sacrilege to receive Jesus while one is in the state of mortal sin. A person in mortal sin should first repent, go to confess to a priest who will give absolution in the name of Christ and the Church, and only then come to the Eucharistic table. The October 2005 Synod of Bishops stressed the importance of the sacrament of Penance for the remission of sins and as a necessary preparatory step for those in mortal sin before they approach the sacred table (cf. prop. 7). Pope Benedict XVI in his catechesis to First Communion children on October 15, 2005, also underlined the role of the sacrament of Penance even for people who have no grave sins because this sacrament strengthens our continued effort to follow Christ with growing fidelity.

Saint Paul urges us to examine our conscience before we receive Holy Communion: "Whoever, therefore, eats the bread or drinks the cup of the Lord in an unworthy manner will be guilty of profaning the Body and Blood of the Lord. Let a man examine himself, and so eat of the bread and drink of the cup. For any one who eats and drinks without discerning the Body eats and drinks judgment upon himself" (1 Cor 11:27–29).

2

THE HOLY EUCHARIST UNITES
HEAVEN AND EARTH

The Holy Eucharist is the mystery of faith in which Christ is
the High Priest. As sacrifice and sacrament, it brings creation
together and offers it to God. The Apocalypse, or the Book
of Revelation, as it is also known, presents a striking imagery
of the heavenly liturgy and helps us appreciate how the Eucharistic celebration, as it were, looks heavenward. At the
same time, the Eucharist commits us to do our part to make
this world a better place in which to live. Indeed, the Eucharist unites heaven and earth and calls for our active faith
response.

Jesus Christ, Our High Priest

If the Eucharist unites heaven and earth, it is mainly thanks to
Jesus Christ. "The Word became flesh, he lived among us"
(Jn 1:14). In the Incarnation, heaven comes down to earth.
As the Church sings in the first Christmas preface, "In the
wonder of the incarnation your eternal Word has brought to
the eyes of faith a new and radiant vision of your glory. In
him we see our God made visible and so are caught up in love
of the God we cannot see" (RM).

On earth as the Incarnate Word, Jesus Christ lifts earth to

heaven by being the victim and the priest in his own redemptive sacrifice. He was already symbolized by the paschal lamb in the exodus (see Ex 12:21–23). John the Baptist pointed him out: "Look, there is the Lamb of God, who takes away the sin of the world" (Jn 1:29). Jesus himself was later to declare that he was freely giving his life for us: "The Father loves me, because I lay down my life in order to take it up again. No one takes it from me" (Jn 10:17). The Apocalypse pays Christ tribute: "Worthy is the Lamb that was sacrificed to receive power, riches, wisdom, strength, honor, glory and blessing" (Rev 5:12).

In the Eucharistic Sacrifice, Christ offers to his beloved bride, the Church, the possibility to be associated with him in offering to the Eternal Father a perfect sacrifice of adoration for the sins of mankind and eloquent petition in the name of Christ. Since he has taken our nature, Jesus associates us with himself in this august mystery. In himself he summarizes, recapitulates, and, in a sense, takes with him all mankind in this supreme act of worship.

In the Eucharist as sacrament, Jesus gives us a pledge of eternal life, a ticket for heaven. We have his own guarantee: "This is the bread which comes down from heaven, so that a man may eat it and not die. I am the living bread which has come down from heaven. Anyone who eats this bread will live for ever, and the bread that I shall give is my flesh for the life of the world" (Jn 6:50–51).

Cosmic Dimension of the Holy Eucharist

It should not escape our attention that, in the Holy Eucharist, Jesus associates with himself not only all mankind but also all creation and offers all to his Eternal Father in the unity of the Holy Spirit.

The Son of God became man "to gather together into one the scattered children of God" (Jn 11:52). By the paschal mystery of his passion, death, and Resurrection he redeemed man.

But the work of redemption goes beyond man in its effects and involves all creation. Original sin turned many created things against man. And man has not always honored God with them, as he should. The whole creation has been awaiting its own redemption, "groaning in labor pains", as Saint Paul puts it (Rom 8:22). "The whole creation is waiting with eagerness for the children of God to be revealed" (Rom 8:19).

Pope John Paul II testified that, as he in his ministry as priest, Bishop, and Pope celebrated the Holy Eucharist in chapels, parish churches, basilicas, lakeshores, seacoasts, public squares, and stadia, he experienced the Eucharist as always in some way celebrated on the altar of the world. The Eucharist embraces and permeates all creation. "The Son of God became man in order to restore all creation, in one supreme act of praise, to the One who made it from nothing. He, the Eternal High Priest who by the blood of his Cross entered the eternal sanctuary, thus gives back to the Creator and Father all creation redeemed" (EE 8).

Saint Paul was already telling the Colossians that the Incarnate Word is the firstborn of all creation and that "God wanted all fullness to be found in him, and through him to reconcile all things to him, everything in heaven and everything on earth, by making peace through his death on the cross" (Col 1:15, 19–20).

And the second Christmas preface says of Christ: "He has come to lift up all things to himself, to restore unity to creation, and to lead mankind from exile into your [the Father's] heavenly kingdom" (RM).

Christ entrusts the celebration of this Eucharistic Sacrifice, with its cosmic dimension, to his Church. At Mass, therefore, mankind, associating with it all creation, offers the supreme act of adoration, praise, and thanksgiving, through Christ, with Christ, and in Christ to the Eternal Father in the unity of the Holy Spirit.

Apocalyptic Imagery of the Heavenly Liturgy

The Book of Revelation speaks in prophetic and apocalyptic language with the Jerusalem temple worship as background. But it also speaks of the Church beginning to spread in the world and presents Jesus Christ as the Gospel Lamb, the King of the universe, the High Priest, the Lord of history, and the immaculate Victim on his throne.

In the Apocalypse, divine worship is praise of heaven begun on earth. The cult images are powerful and clearly liturgical. We see, for example, adoration of the immolated Lamb on his throne, hymns and canticles, acclamations of the crowds of the elect dressed in white, descent of the Church of heaven to earth, the Jerusalem of which the Lord Jesus is the temple. And the people are priestly and royal. The visions recall many cult elements: seven candlesticks, the long white robe of the Son of Man, the white dress of the old men and of the saints, the altar, the Amen, and the exultant Alleluia.

At the same time the Book of Revelation also describes the fight between hell and the faithful of Christ, between the Woman with her children and the Beast, the false prophet who would do all in his power to seduce the inhabitants of the world.

The Eucharist is linked with this heavenly liturgy and, if

well celebrated and lived on earth, will inaugurate the reign of God and dismiss the Devil and his angels.

The Celebrants of the Heavenly Liturgy

The *Catechism of the Catholic Church* speaks of "the celebrants of the heavenly liturgy" (CCC 1137).

Christ crucified and risen is the Lamb "standing as though it had been slain". He is the one High Priest of the true sanctuary. The river of the water of life from the throne of God and of the Lamb is a symbol of the Holy Spirit.

"Recapitulated in Christ", these are the participants in the service of the praise of God in the heavenly liturgy: the heavenly powers, all creation (the four living beings), the servants of the Old and New Covenants (the twenty-four elders), the new people of God (the 144,000), especially the martyrs slain for the Word of God, and the all-holy Mother of God (the Woman), the Bride of the Lamb, and finally a great multitude that no one could number, from every nation, from all tribes and peoples and tongues (see CCC 1137–38; Rev passim).

"What you have come to is Mount Zion and the city of the living God, the heavenly Jerusalem where the millions of angels have gathered for the festival, with the whole Church of first-born sons, enrolled as citizens of heaven" (Heb 12:22–23).

Let us now look further into how the Holy Eucharist celebrated here on earth shows its awareness of its link with the heavenly liturgy.

In Union with the Heavenly Host

The Church in celebrating the Eucharistic Sacrifice is very aware of doing so in union with the heavenly host. One

Eucharistic Prayer after another confesses: "In union with the whole Church we honor Mary, the ever-virgin Mother of Jesus Christ our Lord and God" (RM, Eucharistic Prayer I). Then the following are named: Saint Joseph, the Apostles, the Martyrs, the confessors, the virgins, and all the saints. "May their merits and prayers", the Church prays, "gain us your constant help and protection" (ibid.). The Eastern Rite Anaphoras, or Eucharistic Prayers, do the same.

The angels are given special mention in the preface. For example: "And so with all the choirs of angels in heaven we proclaim your glory and join in their unending hymn of praise" (Advent I). "In our unending joy we echo on earth the song of the angels in heaven as they praise your glory for ever" (II Sunday of Lent). "With thankful praise, in company with the angels, we glorify the wonders of your power" (III Sunday of Lent).

These references to the angels are only natural, as the cry of "Holy, Holy, Holy" that we make our own immediately afterward is attributed by Scripture to them (see Is 6:2; Rev 4:8).

The Church suffering in purgatory is not forgotten. The Eucharistic Sacrifice is also offered for the faithful departed who "have died in Christ but are not yet wholly purified" (Council of Trent, DS 1743), so that they may be able to enter into the light and peace of Christ (see CCC 1371).

It follows therefore that at the Mass "our union with the Church in heaven is put into effect in the noblest manner when with common rejoicing we celebrate together the praise of the divine Majesty" (LG 50). "In the earthly liturgy, by way of foretaste, we share in that heavenly liturgy which is celebrated in the holy city of Jerusalem toward which we journey as pilgrims" (SC 8; see also 1 Cor 15:28; CCC 1090, 1326).

Eschatological Dimension of the Holy Eucharist

The Holy Eucharist leads us to tend toward the life to come. "When you eat this bread, then, and drink this cup, you are proclaiming the Lord's death until he comes", Saint Paul tells the Corinthians (1 Cor 11:26). Christ promised his Apostles his own joy so that their joy might be complete (cf. Jn 15:11). The Eucharist is a foretaste of this joy. It is a confident waiting "in joyful hope for the coming of our Savior, Jesus Christ" (RM, embolism after the Lord's Prayer).

When we receive Jesus in Holy Communion, we are given a pledge of eternal life, of our bodily resurrection, since Jesus promised that those who so receive him in this sacrament have eternal life and that he will raise them up at the last day (see Jn 6:54). Therefore Saint Ignatius of Antioch called Holy Communion "a medicine of immortality, an antidote to death".[1] When, therefore, the priest says to us before the preface: "Lift up your hearts", let us also think of the future life, of heaven, to which the Eucharist is bringing us. Pope John Paul II put it beautifully: "The Eucharist is truly a glimpse of heaven appearing on earth. It is a glorious ray of the heavenly Jerusalem which pierces the clouds of our history and lights up our journey" (EE 19). "Come, Lord Jesus" (Rev 22:20). "The Spirit and the Bride say, 'Come!' Let everyone who listens answer, 'Come'" (Rev 22:17).

Eucharist and Commitment to This World

The fact that the Eucharist brings us to long for, to strain or tend toward the world to come must not be interpreted to

---

[1] Saint Ignatius of Antioch, *Ad Ephesios*, 20 (PG 5, 661); quoted in EE 18; see also SC 47.

imply a diminishing of interest in the improvement of this present world on earth. Quite the contrary.

At the end of Mass the deacon or priest says to us: "Ite, Missa est." "Go, our celebration is ended. You are now sent to go and live what we have prayed and sung and heard. Go to serve God and your neighbor."

The Second Vatican Council is clear on this commitment to improve the earth:

> The expectation of a new earth must not weaken but rather stimulate our concern for cultivating this one. For here grows the body of a new human family, a body which even now is able to give some kind of foreshadowing of the new age. Earthly progress must be carefully distinguished from the growth of Christ's kingdom. Nevertheless, to the extent that the former can contribute to the better ordering of human society, it is of vital concern to the kingdom of God. (GS 39)

Therefore the Holy Eucharist commits us to undertake initiatives to promote development, justice, and peace. Solidarity and cooperation should replace competition and domination. Oppression, repression, or exploitation of individuals or of the poorer minorities or countries should be eliminated. The Christian who is coming from the Eucharistic celebration should examine his conscience on what can or should be done for the poor, the sick, the handicapped, and the needy in general.

Christ washed the feet of his Apostles to teach them that the Holy Eucharist sends us to love our neighbor actively (cf. Jn 13). Saint Paul tells the Corinthians that their participation in the Holy Eucharist is defective if they are indifferent toward the poor (see 1 Cor 11:17–22, 27–34). The recent Instruction of the Congregation for Divine Worship and the

Discipline of the Sacraments stresses this dimension of our participation in the Eucharistic celebration:

> The offerings that Christ's faithful are accustomed to present for the Liturgy of the Eucharist in Holy Mass are not necessarily limited to bread and wine for the eucharistic celebration, but may also include gifts given by the faithful in the form of money or other things for the sake of charity toward the poor. Moreover, external gifts must always be a visible expression of that true gift that God expects from us: a contrite heart, the love of God and neighbor by which we are conformed to the sacrifice of Christ, who offered himself for us. (RS 70)

The October 2005 Synod of Bishops spoke of the Holy Eucharist and the offering of human work. It said that the bread and wine, fruits of the earth and of human work, are presented by us at the altar as an expression of the offering of the life of the human family. They signify that all creation is assumed by Christ the Redeemer in order to be transformed in his recapitulatory love and presented to the Father. Thus is put in evidence the dignity of human work, because through the Eucharistic celebration it is intimately united to the saving sacrifice of Christ the Lord (see prop. 20).

There is no doubt that the Holy Eucharist commits us to strive to make this world a better place in which to live (see EE 20).

Earth Unites with Heaven

We adore, praise, and thank our Lord Jesus Christ, who has given us the possibility and honor of being associated with him in the offering of the Eucharistic Sacrifice. We pray that he will teach us to offer ourselves at Mass through him and with him, to make of us an everlasting gift to God the Father (see RM, Eucharistic Prayer III). Then the Eucharistic Sacrifice becomes for each of us the center of our day and our week, in which we will all be like an offertory procession. The Eucharist teaches the Church to offer herself. As Saint Augustine says: "The Church continues to reproduce this sacrifice in the sacrament of the altar so well-known to believers wherein it is evident to them that in what she offers she herself is offered."[2]

The Holy Eucharist calls on us to be the voice of creation in offering it all to God. The family, work, science and culture, politics and government, the mass media and recreation, plus sun, moon, trees, rivers, and all created things, should all be offered to God. All creation, redeemed by Christ, should be symbolically offered to God in the Eucharistic Sacrifice.

We celebrate the Mass in union with the Blessed Virgin Mary, the angels, and the saints. We pray for the souls suffering in purgatory. We look heavenward to the time when all those redeemed by Christ will be together to sing for eternity the praises of the Father, the Son, and the Holy Spirit.

---

[2] Saint Augustine, *De Civitate Dei* 10, 6 (PL 41, 283); CCC 1372.

3

REVERENCE DUE
TO THE HOLY EUCHARIST

The celebration of the Eucharistic mystery will not be done
well unless the followers of Christ demonstrate reverence
based on sound Eucharistic faith.

Religious Reverence

Reverence is that virtue that inclines a person to show honor
and respect primarily to God, but also to one's parents, to
civil authorities, and to religious leaders. Here we are concerned with reverence to God, in the person of Jesus Christ
in the august sacrifice and sacrament of the Holy Eucharist.

God is holy. He is all holy. "Holy, holy, holy is Yahweh
Sabaoth. His glory fills the whole earth", sing the seraphim
before God's throne (Is 6:3). He is holiness itself. He is
transcendent. He dwells in light unapproachable (see 1 Tim
6:16).

It is part of the virtue of religion to show reverence to
God, to respect his name, and to honor everything connected with him: persons, places, or objects. Cardinal Newman emphasizes the importance of this reverential stance
before God:

Are these feelings of fear and awe Christian feelings or
not? . . . I say this, then, which I think no one can reasonably

32

dispute. They are the class of feelings we *should* have—yes, have to an intense degree—if we literally had the sight of Almighty God; therefore they are the class of feelings which we shall have, *if* we realize His Presence. In proportion as we believe that He is present, we shall have them; and not to have them, is not to realize, not to believe that He is present.[1]

This reverence is due to God, Father, Son, and Holy Spirit. Therefore to Jesus Christ is due our reverence in Bethlehem, at the Lake of Galilee, on the Cross, and in the Holy Eucharist.

Eucharistic Faith, Foundation for Reverence

Catholic faith in the Holy Eucharist is the foundation for reverence for this sacrifice and sacrament. The Second Vatican Council summarizes our faith in the Holy Eucharist as follows:

> At the Last Supper, on the night when he was betrayed, our Savior instituted the Eucharistic Sacrifice of his Body and Blood. He did this in order to perpetuate the sacrifice of the Cross throughout the centuries until he should come again, and so to entrust to his beloved spouse, the Church, a memorial of his death and resurrection: a sacrament of love, a sign of unity, a bond of charity, a paschal banquet "in which Christ is consumed, the mind is filled with grace, and a pledge of future glory is given to us." (SC 47)

This rock foundation that is our faith explains why the Church adores Jesus Christ in the Holy Eucharist. This is adoration, the cult of *latria*, the supreme act of worship due

---

[1] John Henry Cardinal Newman, *Parochial and Plain Sermons* V, 2 (London: Longmans, Green and Co., 1907), 21–22; quoted in CCC 2144.

to God alone. "In the liturgy of the Mass we express our faith in the real presence of Christ under the species of bread and wine by, among other ways, genuflecting or bowing deeply as a sign of adoration of the Lord" (CCC 1378). We recall the great hymn of Saint Thomas Aquinas:

> O Godhead hid, devoutly I adore you,
> Who truly are within the forms before me;
> To you my heart I bow with bended knee,
> As failing quite in contemplating you.
>
> Sight, touch and taste in you are each deceived;
> The ear alone most safely is believed:
> I believe all the Son of God has spoken,
> Than truth's own word there is no truer token.

The Church holds on to this faith without wavering. The same Angelic Doctor teaches us in the *Lauda Sion Salvatorem*:

> This faith to Christian men is given—
> Bread is made flesh by words from heaven:
> Into his blood the wine is turned:
> What though it baffles nature's powers
> Of sense and sight? This faith of ours
> Proves more than nature e'er discerned.

For due reverence to the Holy Eucharist, every Catholic needs proper initiation into this faith and continued growth in it. The Second Vatican Council, teaching on divine revelation and our duty to believe, takes up Saint Paul's phrase: " 'The obedience of faith' (Rom 16:26; cf. 1:5; 2 Cor 10:5–6) must be given to God who reveals, an obedience by which man entrusts his whole self freely to God, offering 'the full submission of intellect and will to God who reveals' (Vatican I, *Dei Filius*, chap. 3, "De Fide", DS 3008) and freely assenting to the truth revealed by him" (DV 5).

Some Catholics are lacking in due reverence to the Holy Eucharist because their Eucharistic faith is poor and full of defects and doubts. Catechesis should not presume that everyone has 100 percent faith. Rather the Catholic faith about the Holy Eucharist should be systematically imparted. Homilies should be solidly based on Holy Scripture, liturgical texts, and other authoritative Church documents. The homily needs special attention because for most Catholics it is the single most effective weekly moment in which they can be fed on the doctrine of the faith to help them know it, love it, and live it with ever greater authenticity. Careful study of the *Catechism of the Catholic Church* and regular reading of reliable Catholic magazines will also help to build up the faith.

The October 2005 Synod of Bishops underlined the importance of solid homilies and ongoing catechesis to nourish the people's Eucharistic faith (see props. 14, 16, 19).

Reverence in the Eucharistic Celebration

The Catholic faith just outlined will show itself in reverence in all matters regarding the Eucharistic celebration, or the Holy Sacrifice of the Mass.

At Mass, the ordained priest acts in the name of Christ. He does not just preside at a prayer assembly like a chairman who conducts a meeting. No. He prays in Christ's name. He preaches with Christ's authority. He consecrates bread and wine in the name and in the person of Christ. He offers Christ to God the Father. He gives the Body and Blood of Christ to God's people, blesses them, and sends them forth to live what they have celebrated.

It matters, therefore, very much that the priest's gestures should be genuine manifestations of Eucharistic faith and love. Although Christ is the chief celebrant, who uses the ministry of the ordained priest as his instrument, the priest's behavior influences the entire congregation.

It is also important that the congregation show reverence. This can manifest itself in their coming early to Mass so that they are recollected when it begins, in their singing, standing, or sitting together when so indicated, and in their maintaining moments of silent prayer. It is sad to see people coming late, reading newspapers during Mass, and conversing freely inside the church as soon as the last blessing is given, as if they were leaving a sports stadium or theatre.

Many congregations do not observe moments of silence, such as after the readings, the homily, or Holy Communion. Sometimes it is the priest who is in a hurry. At other times it is the choir that wants to fill up every quiet moment with singing. And in some cases it is the people in the pew who find moments of silence difficult to observe, because they have not learned to engage in personal interior prayer.

The danger of horizontalism is very real in many Eucharistic celebrations. Some priests and people behave as if they come to Mass primarily to meet one another, to reaffirm one another, and at times even to entertain one another. No, such horizontalism is misplaced. We come to Mass primarily to adore God, to thank him, to ask pardon for our sins, and to make requests for our needs. We are not the center. God is.

Since we are body and soul, our reverence for Jesus in the Holy Eucharist has to show itself also in gestures such as genuflection to the tabernacle when we enter and leave the church, genuflection where prescribed by Church books inside the Mass, genuflection or a bow at the reception of Holy Communion, clean and well-maintained altar furnishings, approved liturgical vestments for the priest and his altar assistants, and a respectful attitude in people coming and going (see prop. 34 of the October Synod of Bishops).

Reverence also includes respect for Church regulations regarding the altar and the sanctuary, the readings and the singing. The music should be suitably approved, and it should show theological, liturgical, and aesthetic beauty and depth. Trite and banal musical productions are not conducive to reverence.

The Church sometimes authorizes extraordinary ministers of Holy Communion to help the priest and deacon when these are not able to cope with the high number of communicants. It is an abuse for the lay faithful to regard service as extraordinary ministers as a power struggle in which they want to prove that they can do what the priest can do. This would be a lack of reverence. It would also be bad theology.

Sometimes we see people desiring to return to the pre-1970 way of celebrating Mass. Generally this is the fault of those who have introduced abuses and their own idiosyncrasies into the Mass, contrary to the clear directives of the Second Vatican Council (see SC 22). If the Mass is celebrated with faith and reverence, and sung also in Latin sometimes, people's Catholic faith and piety will be adequately nourished.

Reverence in the Reception of the Holy Eucharist

The individual Catholic who receives Jesus in the sacrament of the Holy Eucharist shows reverence in many ways.

The most important proof of a communicant's reverence is given by his being in a state of grace. Any Catholic who is unfortunately in the state of mortal sin is bound to go to confession and receive absolution before approaching the Eucharistic table. The Council of Trent declared that it is necessary "by divine decree to confess each and every mortal sin" (Council of Trent, DS 1680). And the 1983 Code of Canon Law says clearly: "Individual and integral confession and absolution are the sole ordinary means by which the faithful, conscious of grave sin, are reconciled with God and the Church; only physical or moral impossibility excuses from such confession, in which case reconciliation can be obtained in other ways" (can. 960). Pope John Paul II, in his April 7, 2002, Apostolic Letter *Misericordia Dei*, requested bishops and priests to do everything possible to make individual access to the sacrament of Penance readily available to the faithful. The Synod of October 2005 repeated this appeal (see prop. 7).

It is therefore to be deplored that in more than one parish, many people regularly go to receive Holy Communion but rarely or ever go to confession. And some of them may be walking around with the weight of mortal sins on their consciences. Some such people are misled by erroneous views that very few people are able to commit a mortal sin or that one lone act cannot be a mortal sin or that they need not bother following the Church's teaching authority when she declares certain actions (such as abortion, contraception, premarital relations, or euthanasia) to be mortal sins but that it is all right just to follow their own consciences. The Catholic who wants to show genuine reverence to the Holy Eucharist will make sure to be in a state of grace before approaching the Eucharistic table.

We also show reverence by the way we receive Holy Communion, kneeling, standing, on the tongue, or in the hand. Even how we dress, how we walk, and how we share in the congregation's acts of singing, standing, sitting, listening, and kneeling can show our faith.

Personal prayer prepares us for proper participation in the

liturgy and helps us to savor its fruits. This applies particularly to the reception of Holy Communion. Bearing in mind that "the sacred liturgy does not exhaust the entire activity of the Church" (SC 9), we appreciate the need for personal reflection and meditation, internal prayer, continuing conversion of heart to God, and ever greater desire of union with Christ. These promote reverence for so great a mystery.

According to personal devotion, a communicant may wish to kneel or to sit in quiet thanksgiving after Communion. Both the priest celebrant and the choir should make room for this. And the diocesan Office for the Sacred Liturgy should not try to regiment movements at all such moments.

Thanksgiving after Mass has traditionally been greatly esteemed in the Church for both the priest and the lay faithful. The missal and the breviary even suggest prayers for the priest before and after the Eucharistic celebration. There is no reason to believe that this is no longer needed. Indeed, in our noisy world of today, such moments of reflective and loving prayers would seem indicated more than ever before. Proposition 34 of the October Synod of Bishops dwells on this. It is a beautiful testimony to hear parishioners say of their pastor: "Father is making his thanksgiving after Mass and will be available to us about ten minutes later." And why should this not be applicable to the congregation, too? Reverence is not automatic. It has to be nurtured, to be built up, to be kept up.

4

LITURGICAL ROLES
IN THE EUCHARISTIC CELEBRATION

The sacred liturgy is the public prayer of the whole Church. The chief person acting in every liturgical celebration is our Lord and Savior Jesus Christ himself, the one perfect Mediator between God and man.

But Christ associates the Church with himself in every liturgical act. Many liturgical acts are hierarchically ordered: with a role for the Bishop and priest, for the deacon, for those lay people who are assigned a liturgical role as defined by the Church, and for all the people of God. The Church in the diocese manifests herself in the most visible way when the Bishop celebrates the Eucharistic Sacrifice in his cathedral church, with the concelebration of his priests, the assistance of the deacons, and the participation of the faithful (cf. SC 41).

Lay Liturgical Roles

For proper celebration of the sacred liturgy and fruitful participation in it by all Christ's faithful, it is important to understand the roles proper to the ministerial or ordained priest and those proper to the lay faithful. Christ is the priest, the

High Priest. He gives all baptized people a share in this role of offering God gifts. The common priesthood of all the baptized gives people the capacity to offer Christian worship, to offer Christ to the Eternal Father through the hands of the ordained priest at the Eucharistic celebration, to receive the sacraments, and to live holy lives, and by self-denial and active charity to make of their entire lives a sacrifice.

The ministerial priest, on the other hand, is a man chosen from among the baptized and ordained by the Bishop in the sacrament of Holy Orders. He alone can consecrate bread into the Body of Christ and wine into the Blood of Christ and offer them to the Eternal Father in the name of Christ and the whole Christian people.[1] It is clear that though they differ from one another in essence and not only in degree, the common priesthood of all the baptized and the ministerial or hierarchical priesthood are closely related (see LG 10).

The major challenge is to help the lay faithful appreciate their dignity as baptized persons. On this follows their role at the Eucharistic Sacrifice and other liturgical acts. They are the people of God. They are insiders. Their role as readers of lessons, as leaders of song, and as the people offering with and through the priest is based on Baptism. The high point is when they communicate at the Eucharistic table. This crowns their participation at the Eucharistic Sacrifice.

There should be no attempt to clericalize the laity. This could happen when, for example, lay people chosen as extraordinary ministers of Holy Communion no longer see this role as being called on to help when the ordinary ministers (bishop, priest, and deacon) are not available in sufficient numbers to cope with the high number of communicants. When the extraordinary ministers see their role as a power

[1] Cf. Council of Trent, *On Ecclesiastical Hierarchy and Ordination* 4, in DS 1767–70.

display to show that what the priest can do, the lay faithful can do too, then we have a problem. How else can we explain the sad error of the lay faithful struggling around the altar to open the tabernacle or to grab the sacred vessels—all against sane liturgical norms and pure good sense?

We have also the opposite mistake of trying to laicize the clergy. When the priest no longer wishes to bless the people with the formula "May Almighty God bless you", but prefers the seemingly democratic wording, "May Almighty God bless us", then we have a confusion of roles. The same thing happens when some priests think they should not concelebrate a Mass but should just participate as lay people in order to show more solidarity with the lay faithful. "In liturgical celebrations", says *Sacrosanctum Concilium*, "whether as a minister or as one of the faithful, each person should perform his role by doing solely and totally what the nature of things and liturgical norms require of him" (SC 28).

A task always to be attended to is the theological, liturgical, and spiritual formation of extraordinary ministers of the Holy Eucharist, of catechists, of other pastoral agents, and of the lay faithful in general. Often mistakes are due, not to bad will, but to lack of knowledge. It is then that the political models of power sharing and power struggle begin to infiltrate the sanctuary. Members of diocesan and national liturgical commissions are to be thanked and encouraged for all they do to bring in more light and, therefore, more harmony. Chapter 12 of this book will go into greater detail on liturgical formation.

The Role of the Diocesan Bishop

The Bishop is endowed with the fullness of the priesthood, of the sacrament of Holy Orders. It is he who ordains priests as cooperators of the episcopal order and deacons for service. The Bishop is the high priest of his flock. "In a certain sense it is from him that the faithful who are under his care derive and maintain their life in Christ" (SC 41). "People should think of us as Christ's servants, stewards entrusted with the mysteries of God" (1 Cor 4:1), says Saint Paul. Indeed, the Bishop should see his offices of teacher and shepherd as ordered toward his office of sanctifier (see LG 26; CD 15; DPMB, no. 76).

It follows that it should be a primary concern of the Bishop that he and his local Church cultivate the worship of God and thus enable the diocese to fulfill its office as the new people of God, a holy nation, a priestly people (see 1 Pet 2: 4–10; LG 10). This is exercised in a special way in liturgical acts, with the Holy Eucharist at the apex. That is where the Bishop is at the height of his service, vocation, sacred power, dignity, and sanctifying role (see LG 21).

The central role of the Bishop is shown especially in what the Council says of him with reference to the Eucharistic celebration. "Every legitimate celebration of the Eucharist is regulated by the Bishop, to whom is committed the office of offering the worship of Christian religion to the divine Majesty and of administering it in accordance with the Lord's commandments and with the Church's laws, as further defined by his particular judgment for his diocese" (LG 26; see also EE 47–52).

The diocesan Bishop is the first steward of the mysteries of God in the particular Church or diocese entrusted to him. He is the moderator, the promoter, and the guardian of the liturgical life of the Church in his diocese. It is he who offers the Eucharistic Sacrifice, or causes it to be offered, so that the Church continually lives and grows (see CD 15; SC 41; CIC can. 387; RS 19).

In his diocese, the Bishop, with due respect for universal Church norms, sees to the regulation, direction, and encouragement of good liturgical celebrations. It is also his duty to explain the reasons for due observance of liturgical norms and to see that the sacred functions are celebrated according to the approved books and that the people are protected from arbitrary innovations. It is therefore his duty to offer correction when necessary.

The diocesan Bishop will find assistance in liturgical commissions if the members are chosen for their proven competence and love for the Church. While he can make specific liturgical norms in his diocese, he should "take care not to allow the removal of that liberty foreseen by the norms of the liturgical books" (RS 21).

In the Latin Church, the Conference of Bishops has a role to play in some liturgical decisions, as recognized by Canon Law and liturgical norms. For example, the Conference may set up regional or national liturgical commissions, arrange for the translation of liturgical texts from the Latin original to the vernacular, submit such texts to the Congregation for Divine Worship and the Discipline of the Sacraments for *recognitio*, and undertake inculturation in understanding with this Congregation (see RM, GIRM 388–99; RS 26–28; VL 31–32).

The Role of the Celebrating Priest

Priests as capable, prudent, and indispensable co-workers of the order of Bishops,[2] are called to the service of the people of God. They constitute one presbyterate around the diocesan Bishop and share one priesthood (*sacerdotium*) with him,

[2] See PO 7; *Pontificale Romanum*, "De Ordinatione Presbyterorum", Praenotanda, 101.

though charged with differing offices. They make the Bishop present in a certain way in each local congregation of the faithful.

A major part of the ministry of the priest refers to how he celebrates the Eucharistic Sacrifice and relates to the Most Blessed Sacrament in the various forms of Eucharistic worship outside Mass.

We all know that the Chief Priest at every Mass is Christ himself. But it is Christ who has decided to make use of the ministry of the ordained priest. It matters very much to the Church, universal and local, how each priest celebrates the Eucharistic Sacrifice. If the priest is obviously full of faith in the Eucharistic mystery, if he is recollected and prayerful, if he handles the Body and Blood of Christ with transparent reverence, and if he respects the liturgical norms of the Church, then blessed is that local community with whom and for whom he offers this sacrifice.

Every priest should be aware that he is part of a glorious tradition. The early Church "remained faithful to the teaching of the apostles, to the brotherhood, to the breaking of bread and to the prayers" (Acts 2:42). The Eucharist is "the principal and central *raison d'être* of the sacrament of the priesthood" (EE 31). The priest is at the height of his calling when he celebrates Mass (see DC 2), because he does so *in persona Christi*.

The Mass is not something we invent, something we put together, something the parish liturgical team fixes up each week! No! The Eucharistic Sacrifice is something we receive in faith, reverence, and thanksgiving. The universal Church is involved in every Mass. The priest is therefore expected to celebrate the sacred rites faithfully according to the approved books and in such a way that his devout celebration manifests the faith of the Church and nourishes the faithful. It follows that he has no authority to add to, or to subtract from, the established rites (see SC 22).

That the priest may carry out creditably his ministry as celebrant of the Eucharist, it follows that he should engage in ongoing study of this mystery so that he can better share with the people "the supreme advantage of knowing Christ Jesus" (Phil 3:8). His personal devotion to Jesus in the tabernacle should be unmistakable. Then every Eucharistic celebration he conducts will be for himself and for the people an experience of faith that is confessed and communicated, of hope that is confirmed, and of charity that is enkindled and spread.

5

ACTIVE PARTICIPATION

In our examination of different roles in the Eucharistic celebration, the necessity for active participation deserves special attention.

Vatican II on Active Participation

A leitmotiv that runs through *Sacrosanctum Concilium* is "active participation" in liturgical celebrations. "Mother Church earnestly desires that all the faithful be led to that full, conscious, and active participation in liturgical celebrations which is demanded by the very nature of the liturgy" (SC 14). The Council goes on to say that this consideration is to be given priority in the liturgical renewal. It states: "In the restoration and promotion of the sacred liturgy, this full and active participation by all the people is the aim to be considered before all else; for it is the primary and indispensable source from which the faithful are to derive the true Christian spirit" (SC 14). *Sacrosanctum Concilium* continues to recall the importance of such participation, for example, in articles 19, 26, 27, 30, 31, 50, and 55.

Active participation is necessary because every liturgical celebration is an action of Christ the priest and of his Body the Church. The Council, therefore, in many parts of *Sacrosanctum Concilium*, refers to the importance of all the faithful being duly involved, such as when it treats liturgical formation of the clergy and people, adaptation and inculturation, communal celebrations, language, more abundant readings from Holy Scripture, the Mass, the sacraments, the Liturgy of the Hours, the liturgical year, and sacred music and art. All is presented in the light of a more conscious and devoted participation and, therefore, with a recognition of the need for proper liturgical formation of priests and of due catechesis of the lay faithful.

"Liturgical services", says the Council, "are not private functions, but are celebrations of the Church, which is the 'sacrament of unity', namely, a holy people united and organized under their Bishops" (SC 26; see also CIC, can. 899, 2). For this reason the Council decrees that communal celebrations that involve the active participation of the faithful are to be preferred to celebrations that are individual and quasi-private (SC 27). Moreover, as previously noted, due observance of roles is to be the norm: "In liturgical celebrations, whether as a minister or as one of the faithful, each person should perform his role by doing solely and totally what the nature of things and liturgical norms require of him" (SC 28).

The Council does not want the people of God to be deprived of this participation, which is variously described as full, active, conscious, interior, exterior, and sacramental (see SC 19, 30).

Basis for Active Participation

Baptism is the primary basis for the active participation of all the faithful of Christ in liturgical celebrations. By this fundamental sacrament of Christian initiation, the Christian people are made "a chosen race, a royal priesthood, a holy nation, a purchased people" (1 Pet 2:9; cf. 2:4–5). By their share in the common priesthood, all the baptized are empowered to take part in Christian worship. At Holy Mass, for example, while the ordained priest, acting in the person of Christ, brings about the Eucharistic Sacrifice and offers it to God in the name of all the people, the faithful for their part join in the offering of the Eucharist by virtue of their royal priesthood (see LG 10). Therefore active participation by all the faithful is not a concession but a right founded on Baptism.

There is a difference in how people take part in the liturgy. It is true that all liturgical celebrations pertain to the whole of the Church, manifest her, and have effects on her. But the Council reminds us that these celebrations "concern individual members of the Church in different ways, according to the diversity of Holy Orders, functions, and degrees of participation" (SC 26).

At the general level of participation are all the baptized. The liturgical assembly is the community of the baptized who "by regeneration and the anointing of the Holy Spirit are consecrated into a spiritual house and a holy priesthood. Thus through all those works befitting Christian people they can offer spiritual sacrifices and proclaim the power of him who has called them out of darkness into his marvelous light (cf. 1 Pet 2:4–10)" (LG 10; see CCC 1141).

But in the Church "the members do not all have the same function" (Rom 12:4). Ordained priests are called by God, in and through the Church, to a special service of the Christian community. They are consecrated by the sacrament of Holy Orders, by which the Holy Spirit enables them to act in the person of Christ the Head, for the service of all the members of the Church. The ministerial priest is at the height of his service at the Eucharistic celebration. The Bishop is the chief priest in his diocese. And deacons are assigned special ministries close to the Bishop and the priest.

There is another title to participation in the sacred liturgy that has to be mentioned. In order to assist the work of the common priesthood of the faithful, other particular ministries also exist. These are not consecrated by the sacrament of Holy Orders. Rather their functions are determined by the Bishops, in accord with liturgical traditions and pastoral needs. These might include servers, lectors, commentators, and members of the choir. "These also exercise a genuine liturgical ministry" (SC 29; see also CCC 1143).

When the needs of the Church require it and the ordained ministers are lacking, lay members of Christ's faithful can also be appointed to supply for certain liturgical offices according to the norm of law. For example, extraordinary ministers of Holy Communion can be appointed in this way (see RS 146–60).

The Earthly Liturgy Reflects the Heavenly One

A major consideration underlining the importance of active participation in the sacred liturgy is the relationship between earth and heaven in the public worship of the Church.

The divine life is that of love, glory, and freedom. Man, created in God's image and redeemed by Christ, is given by God the possibility of participating in the divine life. This redemptive grace reaches people especially through the sacraments when celebrated, participated in, and faithfully lived out.

It is the sacred liturgy that in a special way makes possible this participation in the divine life. Liturgical celebration postulates, makes possible, and increases the indwelling of the

Blessed Trinity in Christ's faithful so that they can the more give glory to the Father, through the Son, in the unity of the Holy Spirit.

Liturgical participation here below on earth tends toward the future, toward heaven. I have already quoted the Second Vatican Council, which said,

> Our union with the Church in heaven is put into effect in the noblest manner when with common rejoicing we celebrate together the praise of the divine majesty. . . . Such is especially the case in the sacred liturgy, where the power of the Holy Spirit acts upon us through sacramental signs. Celebrating the Eucharistic Sacrifice, therefore, we are most closely united to the worshipping Church in heaven as we join with and venerate the memory first of all of the glorious ever-Virgin Mary, of Blessed Joseph and the blessed apostles and martyrs, and of all the saints. (LG 50)

The *Catechism* states the same comforting truth: "By the Eucharistic celebration we already unite ourselves with the heavenly liturgy and anticipate eternal life, when God will be all in all" (CCC 1326).

When, therefore, we talk of active participation in the sacred liturgy, we are speaking of the part that the baptized have in the celebration here on earth, which is related to the heavenly liturgy. Liturgical participation will find its eventual conclusion at the end of our earthly sojourn, for each of us, and at the end of the world for the entire Church. Who does not appreciate the importance of such participation? Are we not thereby striving to contribute our part so that the will of God may be done on earth as it is done in heaven? "Where God's will is done," said Cardinal Ratzinger, "there is heaven, there earth becomes heaven. Surrendering ourselves to the action of God, so that we in our turn may cooperate with him—that is what begins in the liturgy and is meant to unfold further beyond it."[1]

Exaggerated "Active Participation"

The liturgical movement did very good service for many decades in preparing the Church for that liturgical renewal which first appeared officially in the Easter Vigil as restored by Pope Pius XII in 1952. The greatest fruit of the liturgical movement was the liturgical renewal as decreed by the Second Vatican Council. The leaders of the liturgical movement were particularly concerned to have the lay faithful become less passive at liturgical celebrations, especially at Holy Mass. Although the Church never expressed this as her intention, from the Council of Trent (1545–1563) on, liturgical celebrations looked more and more like actions of the clergy at which the laity were present. The Second Vatican Council made a great and successful effort to redress that impression.

Not surprisingly, soon after this Council some people began to exaggerate "active participation" to the extreme of activism. They seemed to be pushing an unwritten agenda of active participation at all costs, in all sorts of ways, by everyone, and in all parts of the liturgy possible. Sometimes this led to noisy celebrations in which the roles of the ordained priesthood and the royal priesthood of the lay faithful were confused. Silence and times for meditative listening were apparently not considered important. Activism, or the effort to get everyone doing something active all the time, was sponsored as if it were what the Sacred Vatican Council had desired (cf. RS 40).

Sometimes such tendencies can be seen in choirs that domi-

[1] J. Ratzinger, *The Spirit of the Liturgy* (San Francisco: Ignatius Press, 2000), p. 176.

nate the celebrations, occupying a position that distracts the congregation and reduces the role of the priest celebrant to one of secondary importance. At other times, activism appears in endless commentaries, where the speaker is probably unconsciously projecting his own self-image and doing his best not to allow the priest or the people to have a quiet moment.

Dance at Mass

A recent craze associated with so-called active participation promotes the idea that there must be dance at a solemn Mass. I have seen a Mass where some misguided person arranged one dance for the entrance procession, another for the *Gloria in Excelsis Deo*, another for the Gospel, one for the offertory, one for the *Sanctus*, one for thanksgiving after Communion, and a final exhibition for the recessional! This dance coordinator neglected to tell us whether people come to Sunday Mass in order to watch dances, whether there is no parish hall for dances after Mass, or whether the Latin Mass liturgy ever had the tradition of dance. Why must the people of God be afflicted with so many distractions when they come just to adore God on Sunday?

To those who want to introduce dancing into the Eucharistic celebration we have to say that such a practice has never been part of the tradition of the Latin Rite liturgy. We have therefore to ask such people to state their case. If they say that their reason is to make the Mass interesting, then our answer must be that we come to Mass to worship God, not to see a spectacle. We have the parish hall and the theatre for such shows.

Others say they welcome dance in order to express their prayer fully, since we are comprised of both body and soul. Our answer must be that the liturgy, indeed, appreciates bodily postures and gestures and has carefully incorporated many of them, such as standing, kneeling, genuflecting, singing, and giving a sign of peace. But the Latin Rite has never included dance.

It is hard for dancers not to draw attention to themselves. While some very refined dances in some cultures can help to elevate the mind, is it not true that for many people dance is a distraction rather than a help to prayer?

Dance easily appeals to the senses and tends to call for approval, enjoyment, a desire for repetition, and a rewarding of the performers with the applause of the audience. Is this what we come to Mass to experience? Have we no theatres and parish halls, presuming that the dance in question is acceptable, which cannot be said of them all?

It is true that in many parts of Africa and Asia there may be a cultural habit of graceful body movement that, with due study and approval by the local Church, may be appropriate within a liturgical celebration. Graceful rhythmical movement has been used in the Ethiopian Rite during the procession for the Gospel. The Roman Rite Mass approved for the Democratic Republic of the Congo has similar movements during the entrance procession.

But this is very different from what the ordinary person in Europe or North America thinks of when the concept of dance is evoked. Can we blame people who associate dance with Saturday evening, a ballroom, theatre, or simply innocent enjoyment? The liturgical books approved by the Bishops and the Holy See for Europe and North America understandably do not authorize the importation of dance into church, let alone into the celebration of the Eucharistic Sacrifice.[2]

---

[2] See the article in the official bulletin of the Congregation for Divine Worship and the Discipline of the Sacraments: *Notitiae* 106–7 (June–July 1975): 202–5.

Grades of Participation

The above considerations lead us to conclude that while the Second Vatican Council ordered fuller, more conscious, and active participation in the liturgy, it is of vital importance that we recognize that the liturgy is primarily something that Christ does, not something that we put together. It is something we receive, not something we invent. It is a celebration of the mysteries of Christ in which we are allowed to take part as members of the Church. "True liturgical education cannot consist in learning and experimenting with external activities. Instead one must be led toward the essential *actio* that makes the liturgy what it is, toward the transforming power of God, who wants, through what happens in the liturgy, to transform us and the world."[3]

Full, active, and conscious participation enables the faithful of Christ to reap more abundant fruit from liturgical celebrations. It enables the salvific event of the celebration of the mysteries of Christ to exert more influence on them. It makes possible for them a deeper share in the divine life that Christ the Savior brought all mankind.

All this means that the better and deeper the participation on the part of a person is, the greater fruit that person will carry away from the liturgy. Let us examine several different possibilities.

Consider the following people taking part at a Eucharistic celebration: an atheist, a malefactor, a person of a religion other than Christian, a Christian in mortal sin, a Christian with attachment to venial sins, a fervent Christian, a saintly Christian, and a Christian mystic well advanced in a life of union with God.

---

[3] Ratzinger, *Spirit of the Liturgy*, p. 175.

Let us imagine that the fictitious people just named all come to Mass. And they mean sincerely to take part. They strive, according to their various states and capacities, to listen, to share with the assembly common postures like standing, sitting, or kneeling, and they try to understand and share what is going on. They know that only the last four named can receive Holy Communion.

What is likely to be the result of their participation? In the final analysis, only God knows. But we can hazard to suppose the following possibilities. The defiant and unbelieving may show no visible change, but grace working secretly in them could arouse healthy curiosity, and no one knows where or how far that might lead. The Christian sinner might obtain at least the beginnings of the actual grace of repentance. The mediocre Christian could be led to more fervent commitment to the faith. The saintly Christian and the mystic would grow in their lives of union with God in ways beyond our observation.

None of this is automatic. Spiritual life and growth are primarily God's work. He it is who takes the initiative. But God ,who created us without our cooperation, will not sanctify and save us without our cooperation.[4] This is another way of saying that our commitment and degree of conscious and active participation in the sacred liturgy do influence the effects of these celebrations in us. Let us now examine some ways in which this participation can manifest itself.

Some External Manifestations of Active Participation

Sacrosanctum Concilium itself lists some of the external manifestations of active participation: acclamations, responses, psalmody, antiphons and songs, as well as actions, gestures, and

---

[4] Cf. Saint Augustine, *Sermo* 169, cap. 2, no. 13 (PL 38, 923).

bodily attitudes (SC 30). The Council said also that "in the revision of liturgical books, it should be carefully provided that the rubrics take the role of the people into account" (SC 31). This has been done in the revised rites these past forty years.

All this is very healthy. Nobody should downplay the importance of these external manifestations. The human being is body and soul. Although interior dispositions are obviously more important, they do not negate the importance of exterior manifestations, because these latter make visible, intensify, and feed the interior requirements. It would be bad psychology and false angelism to ignore the importance of exterior manifestations.

Implicit in all this is the fact that liturgical celebrations should be devoted, faith-filled, and artistically of high quality. The sacred music, the quality of the Scripture proclamation, the altar furnishings, sacred vestments, and provision for the congregation to sit and kneel—each has its importance.

On the other hand, over-regimentation of the congregation, such as unconditional and strict requirements for kneeling or standing when this is not required by approved rubrics, should be avoided. Unity in posture by the congregation is a good thing. All things being equal, it should take precedence over private inclination or arbitrary choice (see GIRM 42). But it is quite another matter when some parish or diocesan officials become rigid or dictatorial and make no concession whatsoever to personal piety, such as a desire to receive Holy Communion on one's knees or the choice to kneel after returning to one's seat.

Interior Dispositions, Silence, and Contemplation

No matter how perfect the external manifestations of active participation may be, the internal dispositions are even more important. *Sacrosanctum Concilium* recognizes this: "In order that the sacred liturgy may produce its full effect, it is necessary that the faithful come to it with proper dispositions, that their thoughts match their words, and that they cooperate with divine grace lest they receive it in vain (cf. 2 Cor 6:1)" (SC 11).

Of fundamental importance are the theological virtues of faith, hope, and charity. Whoever is making progress in these basic attitudes of openness to God is making a better inner preparation for liturgical participation. And to these virtues should be added the virtue of religion and consequent piety, which makes us devoted to God, who is our Father but also our Creator and Judge.

Listening is not a passive affair. It is active openness to God's action in us. It makes us ready to receive the Word of God proclaimed in the liturgical assembly. It leads us to listen to the homily as it applies the sacred readings to the realities and challenges of life on earth today. Listening also includes reverent attention as the priest says or sings the prayers and the preface at Mass and recites the Eucharistic Prayers. Listening, moreover, includes obedience to the directives given by the deacon or other authorized person in the worshipping assembly.

Silence has its place and importance as a help toward the promotion of the required internal dispositions. "At the proper times all should observe a reverent silence" (SC 30). "For in the liturgy God speaks to his people and Christ is still proclaiming his Gospel" (SC 33). The purpose of silence depends on the time it occurs in each part of a celebration.

Within the Act of Penitence at the beginning of Mass and again after the invitation to prayer at Mass and other liturgical celebrations, a period of silence serves as a call to recollection. After the readings and the homily, a suitable pause can help people to meditate on and internalize what they have heard. After Holy Communion, silence serves to allow people to praise God and pray to him in their hearts (see GIRM 45).

A period of silence before liturgical celebrations is a help to recollection. It has, for example, been traditional in the Latin Missal to include in the appendix some prayers recommended to the priest before and after Mass. We are often rather distracted by many things in life. We need a space between our daily activities and our celebration of the sacred rites in order to help us cut out, or at least reduce, the noise of the world without.

Also conducive to contemplation in the celebration of Mass is careful preparation by the priest celebrant, his assistants, the sacristan, the readers, and the choir. Conversely, nervous movements, undue running about, and an endless looking for the proper page are avoided because they cause distractions and make the celebration less dignified. If actors in secular theatres put in long hours of preparation, much more is expected from participants in the celebration of the mysteries of Christ.

While, therefore, we promote active participation, let us recall again that the liturgy is primarily the action of Christ, not ours. "Nothing of what we do in the Liturgy can appear more important than what in an unseen but real manner Christ accomplishes by the power of his Spirit. A faith alive in charity, adoration, praise of the Father and silent contemplation will always be the prime objective of liturgical and pastoral care" (VQA 10).

We live in an age of high technology and a quick-fix mentality. But this propensity should not be allowed to do damage to a contemplative attitude in the liturgy. Every liturgical celebration should provide moments for silence, personal prayer, and contemplative openness to God.

6

LITURGICAL CHANGES IN THE
CELEBRATION OF
THE HOLY EUCHARIST

As human beings we are to a great extent creatures of habit.
We get accustomed to a way of doing things. This is even
more true of a worshipping congregation. And since the
Holy Eucharist is at the center of the prayer life of the
Church (see EE 3), it is no surprise if many people are concerned about changes in the details of the Eucharistic celebration. This matter therefore deserves our consideration.

Why Any Liturgical Change at All?

Let us start with the fundamental question of why there
should be any changes at all in the sacred liturgy.

The liturgy is made up of the rites of the seven sacraments,
the sacramentals (or rites instituted by the Church), and the
Liturgy of the Hours, or the prayers of the Church for
the different hours in the day. Jesus Christ himself instituted
the sacraments: " 'Adhering to the teaching of the Holy
Scriptures, to the apostolic traditions, and to the consensus
. . . of the Fathers' we profess that 'the sacraments of the new
law were . . . all instituted by Jesus Christ our Lord' " (Council of Trent [1547]: DS 1600–1601; CCC 1114). But this

divine institution refers only to the essence of the sacraments, not to the detailed rites with which they are celebrated. Thus Jesus instituted the Eucharistic Sacrifice. But no one will deny that such parts of the rite as the entrance antiphon, penitential rite, opening prayer, and Scripture readings have been arranged by the Church under the guidance of the Holy Spirit across the centuries. What is of divine institution is not subject to change. What is of ecclesiastical arrangement can change. The variety existing between the Latin Rites and those of the Oriental Churches is one proof of this (see OE 6).

The Church, however, does not introduce liturgical change in a careless manner. She is aware that when she celebrates the sacraments, she confesses the faith received from the Apostles. The ancient saying *lex orandi, lex credendi*, or *legem credendi lex statuat supplicanti* (credited to Prosper of Aquitaine of the fifth century, *Ep.* 8) really means that the law of prayer is the law of faith. The Church believes as she prays. The liturgy is a constitutive element of the holy and living tradition (see DV 8). That is why the Church does not allow the minister or the community to modify or manipulate any sacramental or even general liturgical rite. "Even the supreme authority in the Church may not change the liturgy arbitrarily, but only in the obedience of faith and with religious respect for the mystery of the liturgy" (CCC 1125).

The Second Vatican Council, wrongly blamed by some people for having introduced too many changes in the liturgy, proceeded very carefully. It says that regulation of the sacred liturgy depends solely on the authority of the Church as exercised by the Apostolic See and, as laws may determine, on the bishop. Territorial bodies of bishops also have some competence. "Absolutely no other person, not even a priest, may add, remove, or change anything in the liturgy on his own authority" (SC 22).

The Council goes on to give guidelines for the legitimate introduction of changes in the liturgy. In order to maintain sound tradition, careful theological, historical, and pastoral study has first to be made regarding any supposedly desirable change. General liturgical forms and structures are to be attended to. There must be no innovations unless the good of the Church genuinely and certainly requires them. And care must be taken that any new forms adopted should in some way grow organically from forms already existing (see SC 23).

One can see that the Second Vatican Council was no iconoclast. It did not order a reckless change of worship patterns dear to Catholic tradition. What cannot, however, be denied is that two good Catholic scholars may agree to the wisdom of the principles laid down by the Council but disagree on how faithful a particular revised rite has been to those principles.

Missals since Trent

The Council of Trent (1545–1563) gave considerable attention to the sacrifice and sacrament of the Holy Eucharist. After that great assembly, Pope Saint Pius V issued a typical edition of the *Roman Missal* in 1570. Saint Pius V was especially concerned with preserving the more recent tradition, then unjustly being assailed (Mass as sacrifice, Real Presence, ministerial priesthood). He introduced only very slight changes to the first printed edition of the *Roman Missal* of 1474, which in turn had been faithful to tradition since Pope Innocent III (1198–1216). This Mass book of Saint Pius V, with minor additions, remained in use for four centuries.

The Second Vatican Council (1962–1965) issued as its first

major document the Constitution on the Sacred Liturgy, *Sacrosanctum Concilium*, on December 4, 1963. As a result of the directives of this Constitution, Pope Paul VI issued the first typical edition of the revised *Roman Missal* in 1970. This missal saw a second typical edition in 1975. What we are now considering is the third typical edition. It was authorized by Pope John Paul II in the Jubilee Year 2000 and came off the Vatican Polyglot Press on February 22, 2002, the Feast of Saint Peter's Chair.

Is this missal in line with the faith and tradition of the Church?

A Witness to Unchanged Faith

The *General Instruction of the Roman Missal* makes clear from its very first paragraph that the current norms and the new missal that the Church of the Roman Rite is to use from now on in the celebration of Holy Mass are "evidence of the great concern of the Church, of her faith, and of her unchanged love for the great mystery of the Eucharist" (GIRM 1).

It is important that we see and receive this missal as a witness of our unchanged Catholic faith. The Church believes, and has always believed, that the Mass is the sacrifice of the Body and Blood of Christ by which Jesus perpetuates the Sacrifice of the Cross throughout the centuries until he should come again. The Sacrifice of the Cross and its sacramental renewal in the Mass are one and the same, differing only in the manner of offering. Consequently, the Mass is at once a sacrifice of praise and thanksgiving, of propitiation and satisfaction (see Council of Trent: DS 1738–59; GIRM 2).

Moreover, the Church firmly believes that Jesus Christ is really present under the Eucharistic species because at the moment of consecration the wonder of transubstantiation takes places: bread and wine become the Body and the Blood of Christ. The Church adores Christ in this Sacrament at Mass and outside Mass, as in Eucharistic processions (see GIRM 3).

The ministerial, or ordained, or hierarchical priest consecrates bread and wine and offers the Body and Blood of Christ to God the Father in the person of Christ. All the baptized, by virtue of their royal or baptismal priesthood, offer with and through the ministerial priest and also learn to make of their lives a spiritual sacrifice (GIRM 4–5).

A Witness to Unchanged Tradition

The GIRM goes into considerable detail to show that the 1970, 1975, and 2002 missals are witnesses to the unchanged tradition of the Church. Paragraph 6 needs quoting in full:

> In setting forth its instructions for the revision of the Order of Mass, the Second Vatican Council, using the same words as did St. Pius V in the Apostolic Constitution *Quo primum*, by which the Missal of Trent was promulgated in 1570, also ordered, among other things, that some rites be restored "to the original norm of the holy Fathers" (SC 50). From the fact that the same words are used it can be seen how both *Roman Missals*, although separated by four centuries, embrace one and the same tradition. Furthermore, if the inner elements of this tradition are reflected upon, it also becomes clear how outstandingly and felicitously the older *Roman Missal* is brought to fulfillment in the new.

This statement of the *General Instruction* is worth noting to help our faith in the Church in every age and to avoid attachment to one moment or year in the history of the Church, to the exclusion of the Church of today and tomorrow, as if the

Holy Spirit ceased to be with the Church in a particular year. Many studies have taken place in our times to help the Church discover more of the "norm of the holy Fathers". Thus the missal of today is enriched with elements new and old (see GIRM 7–9), including many beautiful prayers drawn from the ancient manuscripts and the writings of the Fathers of the Church, such as Saint Leo the Great and Saint Gregory, and others that draw on the documents of the Council itself.

Accommodation to New Conditions

The *General Instruction* explains how fidelity to the "norm of the holy Fathers" requires of us not only preservation of what our immediate forebears have passed on to us, but also an understanding of the Church's entire history, how the one Catholic faith has lived and has been celebrated in the Semitic, Greek, and Latin areas, and how the Holy Spirit guides the Church in our present-day world of growing cultural plurality (see GIRM 9). Thus the Church "while remaining faithful to her office as teacher of truth safeguarding 'things old', that is, the deposit of tradition, fulfills at the same time another duty, that of examining and prudently bringing forth 'things new' (cf. Mt 13:52)" (GIRM 15). In many respects, the liturgical norms of the Council of Trent have been completed and perfected by those of the Second Vatican Council. (I discuss this important and complex topic more fully in the next chapter.)

Some Outstanding Features

I might selectively mention here a few features of the third typical edition of the *Roman Missal*.

The Prayer of the Faithful was restored to the Eucharistic celebration by the Second Vatican Council (see SC 53). It is the people's response in a certain way to the Word of God that they have welcomed in faith. They exercise their baptismal priesthood and offer prayers to God for the salvation of all (see 1 Tim 2:1–2). While reasonable freedom of expression is allowed in its formulation, the following four major intentions should generally be prominent:

The needs of the Church
Public authorities and the whole world
Those in suffering or difficulty
The local community (see GIRM 69–71)

Compositions of intentions should be sober and theologically acceptable. While priests, deacons, and experienced religious and pastoral workers can generally be trusted to compose suitable intentions on the spot, it is best that the pastor or other rector of the church oversee written scripts before Mass to avoid embarrassments during the sacred celebration and to see that the intentions are articulated in the proper, prudent style and with the brevity (GIRM 71) that is a mark of the Roman Rite.

The *preface* is the hymn of thanksgiving to God sung or proclaimed by the priest celebrant as an introduction to the Eucharistic Prayer. If we exclude duplicates and the prefaces attached to some Eucharistic Prayers, there are more than ninety prefaces listed in the 2002 missal (pages 1307–10 of the Latin missal). No missal of the Roman Rite, for some thousand years, ever had such a rich variety. It should be added, however, that the Ambrosian and Mozarabic Rites have still many more, and the ancient Roman books had hundreds.

There are quite a number of *Eucharistic Prayers* in this missal—thirteen. The best known, sometimes called Eucharistic

Prayer I, is the ancient Roman Canon. For centuries it was the sole Eucharistic Prayer of the Roman Church. Eucharistic Prayers II, III, and IV were added in 1968. With a total of thirteen masterpieces in the 2002 missal, one wonders why a priest would still want to invent one of his own against all common sense, liturgical norms (see SC 22), and the clear injunction of *Ecclesia de Eucharistia*, no. 52.

Masses for Various Circumstances have been increased.

> Since the liturgy of the Sacraments and Sacramentals covers, for the faithful who are properly disposed, almost every event in life to be sanctified by divine grace that flows from the paschal mystery, and because the Eucharist is the Sacrament of Sacraments, the Missal provides formularies for Masses and orations that may be used in the various circumstances of Christian life, for the needs of the whole world or for the needs of the Church, whether universal or local. (GIRM 368)

Is it not a pity that in many parishes not many of these Masses are celebrated except Masses for the Dead? The rich catechetical doctrine in them is very nourishing. Particularly on days in Ordinary Time when there is no obligatory memorial, many of these Masses would be allowed.

Action by the Liturgical Assembly

Among the many actions that the missal underlines as expected from the liturgical assembly, four can be examined.

Singing has great importance in the liturgical celebration. Saint Paul tells us to sing together psalms, hymns, and spiritual songs (see Col 3:16). Gregorian chant is proper to the Roman liturgy. Other types of sacred music, such as polyphony and religious music according to local culture, also have their place. They should be approved by Church authority (see GIRM 39–41).

Movements and postures help to adorn a liturgical celebration with beauty and noble simplicity. A common posture, observed by all the participants as far as possible, is a sign of the unity of the members of the Christian community gathered for the sacred liturgy. It both expresses and fosters the intention and spiritual attitude of the participants. Attempts should not be made to specify the posture of the faithful to the point of appearing to regiment the people of God (see GIRM 42–44).

Silence has its place in the liturgical celebration. It can help people to become recollected. It can favor reflection after the reading or the homily. It provides space after Holy Communion to allow people to pray to God in their hearts (see GIRM 45).

The Sign of Peace is extended shortly before Holy Communion. "According to the tradition of the Roman Rite, this practice does not have the connotation either of reconciliation or of a remission of sins, but instead signifies peace, communion and charity before the reception of the Most Holy Eucharist" (RS 71; GIRM 82, 154). People should just greet the people nearest to them and not walk around.

With reference to liturgical changes, therefore, all of us need faith in the Church, which convinces us that she is led by the Holy Spirit. And we should show our love for the Church by observing her norms for Eucharistic and other liturgical worship. The freedom of people to suggest a modification or change or to advise that there be no change in this or that ritual remains intact. Such suggestions should be sent to the proper Church authority. They might help to produce better texts or rituals. What is not correct is to take the liturgical law into one's own hands and to push one's choices or idiosyncrasies onto the public worship of the Church.

7

ADAPTATION AND INCULTURATION IN THE EUCHARISTIC CELEBRATION

Adaptation and inculturation concern the entire life of the Church in a given place, the expression of the Gospel in a cultural situation. They are most visible in matters liturgical, especially with reference to the Eucharistic celebration. Here we are focusing on adaptation and inculturation in matters touching Holy Mass.

General Directives of Vatican II

The general directives on adaptation and inculturation are given by the Second Vatican Council in its very first document, *Sacrosanctum Concilium*. They are directives, however, of careful openness.

> Even in the liturgy [the Council says] the Church has no wish to impose a rigid uniformity in matters which do not involve faith or the good of the whole community. Rather she respects and fosters the spiritual adornments and gifts of the various races and peoples. Anything in their way of life that is not indissolubly bound up with superstition and error she studies with sympathy and, if possible, preserves intact. Sometimes in fact she admits such things into the liturgy itself, as long as they harmonize with its true and authentic spirit. (SC 37)

This fundamental directive is one to which reference has to be made again and again. It respects both the unity of the Catholic faith and the positive elements with which God has gifted all cultures.

The Council wanted the substantial unity of the Roman Rite to be maintained. Given that safeguard, it wanted liturgical books to allow for legitimate variations and adaptations to different groups, regions, and peoples, especially in what were in those days considered mission lands. It even speaks of possible structuring of rites and devising of rubrics (see SC 38). This will become clearer as these reflections unfold.

The intentions of the Council were, in the first place, implemented in the way in which the revised Latin *editiones typicae* were drawn up, mostly in the late 1960s and the 1970s. The new texts differed at many points from the books current before the Council in that they allowed some built-in flexibility and choice that was left to the celebrant to make use of according to his pastoral judgment. This provision in the liturgical books for the taking of on-the-spot options by the priest is in the Latin text of some of the liturgical legislation referred to as *accommodatio*, for which there is no easy equivalent in English and so tends to be called "adaptation". Another level of flexibility provided by the liturgical books concerns those things that are explicitly left to the decision of the Bishops' Conference at the moment when vernacular translations are prepared.

The Diocesan Bishop

The diocesan Bishop is the high priest of his flock. The life in Christ of the faithful under his care in a certain sense derives from him and depends upon him (see SC 41).

The Bishop is therefore to promote, regulate, and be vigilant over the liturgical life in his diocese. If we take the important example of the missal and the celebration of Mass, he regulates the discipline of concelebration (see GIRM 202) and establishes norms regarding the office of those who serve the priest at the altar (see GIRM 107), the distribution of Holy Communion under both species (see GIRM 283), and the construction and ordering of churches (see GIRM 291). Above all, it is the responsibility of the Bishop to foster the spirit of the sacred liturgy in his priests, deacons, and lay faithful (see GIRM 387). In fostering a true sense of the liturgy, he does not forget those things that are left in particular not only to the celebrant, but also to some degree to those who assist the priest in different ways, so that they will make intelligent and suitable use of the options that are left to their free choice in the liturgical books. When something goes wrong, he moves things back on track.

The Bishops' Conference

If the Bishop's role in his diocese is one of regulation, his responsibilities clearly extend more widely to the good of the entire Church and, in particular, to the faithful of the country in which he ministers. It is here that we may speak of those things that are adaptations properly so called and that go beyond the boundaries of a diocese and by their nature demand a wider degree of coordination. Such things are placed, in accord with the norm of law, within the competence of a Bishops' Conference (see GIRM 388). Here are some examples.

It is the competence of the Conference of Bishops to prepare and approve an edition of the *Roman Missal* in the authorized local languages and obtain the required *recognitio* from the Apostolic See. It is up to the Conference of Bishops to decide on adaptations indicated in the *General Instruction* and in the Order of Mass and to obtain for them the *recognitio*. Examples are:

- the gestures and postures of the faithful (see GIRM 43);

- the gestures of veneration toward the altar and the Book of the Gospels (see GIRM 273);

- the texts of chants at the entrance, the presentation of gifts, and at Communion (see GIRM 48, 74, 87);

- the readings from Sacred Scripture to be used in special circumstances (see GIRM 362);

- the form of the gesture of peace (see GIRM 82);

- the manner of receiving Holy Communion (see GIRM 160, 283);

- the materials for the altar and sacred furnishings, especially the sacred vessels and the vestments (see GIRM 301, 326, 329, 339, 342–46).

There are similar lists in the opening sections of all the liturgical books, detailing the things that the Bishops' Conference may change in the normal course of events when they prepare the local vernacular editions (see VL 55).

"The first significant measure of inculturation is the translation of liturgical books into the language of the people" (VL 53; see also SC 36, 54, 63). It makes little sense to talk of inculturation if the people do not even have the liturgical texts available in an approved translation that has obtained the *recognitio*. Translation is one of the major roles of a Bishops' Conference (see GIRM 392).

Sacred Scripture has a key place and importance in the

liturgy. From it the readings are taken, the homily is based on it, and from it the psalms are sung. Moreover, prayers, orations, and liturgical songs are inspired by it and therefore need to reflect its wording. The Conference of Bishops has the important task of providing proper translations of the Bible. Indeed, *Varietates Legitimae* does not hesitate to say that "the translation of the Bible, or at least of the biblical texts used in the liturgy, is the first necessary step in the process of the inculturation of the liturgy" (VL 28; see also GIRM 391).

The Conference of Bishops also sees to matters regarding musical settings for liturgical use as well as musical instruments (see GIRM 393).

While each diocese prepares its own Calendar and Proper of Masses, the Bishops' Conference assumes this role as regards the Calendars and Liturgical Propers of the nation, in either case with the formal approbation of the Holy See (see GIRM 394).

Bishops' Conferences will find that a great deal can be done in making liturgical celebrations more congenial to the people, from a cultural point of view, without thinking of changing essential rites and texts. If, for example, a new church is built to reflect local architectural styles, if artwork and decoration on vestments or if Stations of the Cross and sacred images reflect local genius, if the music respects the nature of the local language and is effective in touching the soul of the people, then much is already accomplished (see VL 39–43). At the same, with the rise of tourism, there may be objects on sale passing for local art but which are really recent inventions for foreign taste and commercial purposes. Discretion will be needed not to incorporate such styles into Church use.

Many African countries have many languages. This poses a

challenge to the Bishops' Conference. *Liturgiam Authenticam*, nos. 10–18, advises Conferences on the criteria needed for selection and adoption of a language for the sacred liturgy. The training and selection of translation experts and financial aspects of the production and distribution of liturgical books are also important considerations.

For Inculturation in the Deeper Sense

The adaptations that have just been discussed are of fundamental importance. But sometimes deeper or more thorough-going adaptation is considered necessary. Let us recapitulate before going forward.

We can speak of three steps, or three grades or categories: *accommodatio*, adaptation, and inculturation.

The simplest form of adaptation treated in the *General Instruction of the Roman Missal* and in the body of the *Roman Missal* is what is entrusted to the priest celebrant. "These adaptations consist for the most part in the choice of certain rites or texts, that is, of the chants, readings, prayers, explanations, and gestures which may respond better to the needs, preparation, and culture of the participants" (GIRM 24; cf. RS 39). The priest has only the faculty to choose from existing approved texts, not to invent, remove, or change anything (see SC 22). We can call this *accommodatio*.

The second grade of adaptations refers to what is placed within the competence of the Conference of Bishops, as has just been discussed.

Inculturation in the strict sense makes heavier demands. It is the third step. If the Bishops consider that the culture and traditions of their people make deeper demands than mere adaptation as hitherto indicated, the Bishops' Conference is to work according to the directives of *Sacrosanctum Concilium*

40; *Ad Gentes* 22; *Varietates Legitimae* 63–69; and, as applied to the case of the missal, the *General Instruction of the Roman Missal* 395–99.

The Essence of Inculturation

The Gospel of our Lord and Savior Jesus Christ is meant for all peoples, languages, and cultures. It should be at home among each people and culture and vice versa.

Inculturation is understood as "the incarnation of the Gospel in autonomous cultures and at the same time the introduction of these cultures into the life of the Church" (SA 21). Inculturation signifies "the intimate transformation of authentic cultural values through their integration in Christianity and the insertion of Christianity in the various human cultures".[1]

The mystery of the Incarnation offers a model, an image, to inculturation. The Son of God took on human nature in a particular culture. The Gospel takes on all that is good, noble, or true in a culture. Some elements it assumes. Others it purifies and elevates. And some elements have to be rejected (see LG 13, 17; AG 9).

"The liturgy, like the Gospel, must respect cultures, but at the same time invite them to purify and sanctify themselves" (VL 19).

Many post–Vatican II Magisterial documents speak of the importance of inculturation. Examples are the Code of Canon Law of the Oriental Churches, can. 584 §2; *Redemptoris Missio* 52–54; *Slavorum Apostoli* 21–22; and *Ecclesia in Asia* 21–22. The October 2005 Synod did not forget the importance of inculturation (see prop. 26).

---

[1] Synod of 1985, Final Report, II, D, 4; cf. REM 52.

First African Synod and Inculturation

The first Special Assembly for Africa of the Synod of Bishops (African Synod, for short), as was to be expected, gave careful attention to the place of inculturation in the evangelization of the continent. It is the process by which "catechesis takes flesh in the various cultures" and is considered an urgent priority in the life of the particular Churches for a firm rooting of the Gospel in Africa (see EA 59).

The Synod recognized inculturation as a difficult and delicate task. So the Synod Fathers said: "Considering the rapid changes in the cultural, social, economic and political domains, our local Churches must be involved in the process of inculturation in an ongoing manner, respecting the two following criteria: compatibility with the Christian message and communion with the universal Church. . . . In all cases, care must be taken to avoid syncretism" (prop. 31, quoted in EA 62).

The Synod understood inculturation as encompassing the whole life of the Church and the whole process of evangelization. Therefore it included theology, liturgy, the Church's life and structures. "Inculturation of the liturgy, provided it does not change the essential elements, should be carried out so that the faithful can better understand and live liturgical celebrations" (prop. 34, quoted in EA 64).

It can therefore be asserted that the First African Synod encouraged inculturation in the sacred liturgy, with all the safeguards as indicated. So did the continental Synods for Asia, Oceania, and America.

Presuppositions before Inculturation Initiatives

It is useful to examine some presuppositions that should be verified in undertaking initiatives for inculturation.

The first requirement is that an Episcopal Conference "has exhausted all the possibilities of adaptation offered by the liturgical books; that it has made an evaluation of the adaptations already introduced and perhaps revised them before proceeding to more far-reaching adaptations" (VL 63).

The goal of inculturation of the Roman Rite as laid down by the Second Vatican Council should be kept in mind. "Both texts and rites should be so drawn up that they express more clearly the holy things they signify and so that the Christian people, as far as possible, may be able to understand them with ease and to take part in the celebration fully and actively and as befits a community" (SC 21; VL 35).

There should be no hasty changes. No innovations should be introduced unless a genuine and certain benefit to the Church requires it. New forms adopted should in some way grow organically from forms already existing (see SC 23; VL 46; GIRM 398).

The substantial unity of the Roman Rite should be maintained. This unity is currently expressed in the typical editions of liturgical books published by the authority of the Supreme Pontiff and in the liturgical books approved by the Episcopal Conferences for their areas and given *recognitio* by the Holy See. The work of inculturation does not foresee the creation of new families of rites (see GIRM 397–99; VL 36).

We might add to these official requirements that inculturation is certainly not to be understood as the covert import of fashionable ideas from other continents. If care is not taken, these could imperceptibly come in through agents of the Gospel from other lands or through nationals who have studied elsewhere.

The proper authority should approve initiatives for inculturation. This means the Apostolic See and, within the limits fixed by law, Episcopal Conferences and the diocesan Bishop.

"Inculturation is not left to the personal initiative of celebrants or to the collective initiative of a congregation" (VL 37).

If all this is observed, the local Church will spare herself many false steps, lamentable innovations, and avoidable confusion and disturbance of the people of God. It now remains for us to spell out the procedure for practical inculturation.

Procedure for Introduction of Inculturated Rites

Clear instructions for the proper introduction of inculturated rites are given in *Varietates Legitimae*, nos. 65–69, and in the *General Instruction of the Roman Missal*, nos. 395–99. These are the indications for the application of no. 40 of *Sacrosanctum Concilium*.

The Episcopal Conference first examines what it considers could be modified or introduced in liturgical celebrations in order to pay more attention to the traditions and mentality of its people. The Conference then asks its national or regional liturgical commission to make a thorough study of the matter and pass on to it its recommendations. Such a commission should assemble the best available experts in liturgy, Scripture, theology, anthropology, history, literature, music, and similar disciplines for a proper study. Where it is considered opportune, the advice of people of other religions could be asked regarding religious or civil meanings of this or that element. If the situation requires it, this preliminary examination will be made in collaboration with the Episcopal Conferences of neighboring territories that have a similar culture (see AG 22; VL 30).

Thereafter, the Bishops' Conference presents its proposal to the Congregation for Divine Worship and the Discipline of the Sacraments. After due examination between the Conference and the Congregation, the latter grants the Episcopal Conference the faculty to make an experiment for a definite period of time, where this is appropriate. Although the documents do not explicitly require it, it might well be prudent to try some experiments only in a limited area or in a number of selected places.

At the end of such controlled experimentation, the Bishops' Conference reexamines the matter to see if any modifications are needed. It then communicates its conclusion to the Congregation for Divine Worship and the Discipline of the Sacraments. This Congregation can still call for some modification before finally issuing a decree to give its consent. The Bishops' Conference will take the needed measures to give due information to the Christian faithful, both clergy and lay faithful, so that changes are not introduced in an abrupt way.

One can see from these indications that it is a terrible abuse of the concept and practice of inculturation to understand it as the product of the fertile imagination of some enthusiast, which is created on Saturday evening and forced down on the innocent congregation on Sunday morning. Inculturation is no do-it-yourself affair. It is a serious matter that affects the prayer life of the Church and therefore her faith, considering the time-honored adage *lex orandi, lex credendi*. And when one considers that the Eucharistic celebration is "the fount and apex of the whole Christian life" (LG 11) and is at the center of the Church's life, then the advice will be stronger and louder to be very careful and not too fast in introducing innovations into the way of celebrating the Holy Eucharist.

8

ON LITURGICAL NORMS

It should cause no surprise to anyone that there are norms for the celebration of the Holy Eucharist. Sound doctrine advises them. Tradition has known them. Customs have introduced some. And common sense is in favor of at least some norms. But sometimes we find that common sense is not very common. It therefore pays to say a word on the place of liturgical norms and the need to observe them.

Reasons for Liturgical Norms

The sacred liturgy is an exercise of the priestly office of Jesus Christ. It is the public worship performed by the Mystical Body of Christ, by the Head and his members (see SC 7).

Liturgical celebrations have some elements that are of divine institution. Such are the essentials of the seven sacraments. There are elements that are of ecclesiastical institution. In deciding on these elements the Church takes great care to be faithful to Holy Scripture, to honor the tradition handed down through the centuries, to manifest her faith and rejoice in it, and to lead all the faithful to worship God, follow the example of Christ, and show love and service of one's neighbor. Between these two we can speak of a third:

namely, those elements of the liturgy that are found from early days in all or almost all of the great liturgical traditions and that must therefore go back at the very least to a period close to the Apostles and perhaps even to our Lord. While we may not have certain knowledge on the matter in a given case, it is a strong reason for avoiding hasty innovation or neglect (see VL 26–27; GIRM 397; LA 4–5; RS 9).

Liturgical celebrations should be experiences of the traditional faith that is confessed, celebrated, and communicated, of hope that is expressed and confirmed, and of charity that is sung and lived.

Since liturgical celebrations are public acts performed in the name of the universal Church, with Jesus Christ himself as the Chief Priest, it follows that as the centuries rolled by, the Church has necessarily developed norms according to which her public worship is to be expressed. Liturgical norms protect this treasure that is Christian worship. They manifest the faith of the Church, promote it, celebrate it, and communicate it. They also manifest the nature of the Church as a hierarchically constituted family, a community of worship, love, and service, and a body that promotes union with God and holiness of life and gives sinners hope of conversion, forgiveness, and new life in Christ.

Moreover, liturgical norms help to protect the celebration of the sacred mysteries, especially the Holy Eucharist, from being damaged by additions or subtractions that do damage to the faith and that may at times risk making a sacramental celebration invalid. The people of God are thus guaranteed celebrations in line with the traditional Catholic faith, and they are not left at the mercy of someone's personal ideas, feelings, theories, or idiosyncrasies.

Pope John Paul II was very insistent on the important role of norms regarding the celebration of the Eucharist. "These norms are a concrete expression of the authentically ecclesial nature of the Eucharist; this is their deepest meaning. Liturgy is never anyone's private property, be it of the celebrant or of the community in which the mysteries are celebrated" (EE 52). Love for the Church leads a person to observe these norms: "Priests who faithfully celebrate Mass according to the liturgical norms, and communities which conform to those norms, quietly but eloquently demonstrate their love for the Church" (ibid.). Our respect for the mysteries of Christ leads us to respect these norms: "No one is permitted to undervalue the mystery entrusted to our hands: it is too great for anyone to feel free to treat it lightly and with disregard for its sacredness and its universality" (ibid.).

In its *Message* the October 2005 Synod of Bishops stressed the same point: "We are convinced that respect for the sacred character of the liturgy is transmitted by genuine fidelity to liturgical norms of legitimate authority. No one should consider himself master of the Church's liturgy. Living faith that recognizes the presence of the Lord is the first condition for beautiful liturgical celebrations which give a genuine 'Amen' to the glory of God" (*Nuntius* 8).

Lex orandi, lex credendi

The sacraments sanctify people, build up the Body of Christ, and give worship to God. Because they are signs, they also instruct. They not only presuppose faith, but by words and objects they also nourish, strengthen, and express it. That is why they are called "sacraments of faith" (see SC 59).

The faith of the Church has expressed itself in how the Church prays and especially in how she celebrates the Holy Eucharist and the other sacraments. There are words and concepts that have acquired a deep meaning in the Church's life, faith, and prayer through the centuries. Examples are Person, Trinity, Divine Majesty, Incarnation, Passion, Resurrection, salvation, merit, grace, intercession, redemption, sin, repentance, forgiveness, propitiation, mercy, penance, reconciliation, Communion, and service. There are gestures and postures that help to express what the Church believes. Examples are the Sign of the Cross, bowing, kneeling, standing, listening, and going in procession.

"The Church's faith precedes the faith of the believer who is invited to adhere to it. When the Church celebrates the sacraments, she confesses the faith received from the apostles" (CCC 1124). This is a strong argument in favor of great care in the wording, gestures, and norms of liturgical celebrations.

The relation between the faith of the Church and her liturgical celebration has been encapsulated in the ancient saying *lex orandi, lex credendi* (the law of prayer is the law of faith), or *legem credendi lex statuat supplicandi* (let the law of prayer determine the norm of faith). This statement of Catholic faith is credited to Prosper of Aquitaine of the fifth century (*Ep.* 8). It is quoted in the *Indiculus* or the *Pseudo-Celestine Chapters*. Pope Celestine reigned from 422 to 432 (see DS 246).

The Church believes as she prays. The liturgy is a constitutive element of the holy and living tradition of the Church (see DV 8). That is why the Church does not allow the minister or the community to modify or manipulate any sacramental or even general liturgical rite. "Even the supreme authority in the Church may not change the liturgy arbitrarily, but only in the obedience of faith and with religious respect for the mystery of the liturgy" (CCC 1125).

Redemptionis Sacramentum is strong on this point:

> The Church herself has no power over those things which were established by Christ himself and which constitute an unchangeable part of the Liturgy. Indeed, if the bond were to

be broken which the Sacraments have with Christ himself who instituted them, and with the events of the Church's founding, it would not be beneficial to the faithful but rather would do them grave harm. For the Sacred Liturgy is quite intimately connected with principles of doctrine, so that the use of unapproved texts and rites necessarily leads either to the attenuation or to the disappearance of that necessary link between the *lex orandi* and the *lex credendi*. (RS 10)

Authority over the Liturgy

The above reflections lead us to ask who has authority over the sacred liturgy. Who decides on the texts, the ceremonies, the norms? We cannot afford to be vague on this.

The Second Vatican Council is not ambiguous: "Regulation of the sacred liturgy depends solely on the authority of the Church, that is, on the Apostolic See and, as laws may determine, on the Bishop. In virtue of power conceded by the law, the regulation of the liturgy within certain defined limits belongs also to various kinds of competent territorial bodies of Bishops legitimately established." Then the Council adds the warning: "Therefore, absolutely no other person, not even a priest, may add, remove, or change anything in the liturgy on his own authority" (SC 22).

These rulings are not a sign of lack of respect for anyone. They follow from the fact that the liturgy is a celebration of the universal Church. "The prayers addressed to God by the priest who presides over the assembly in the person of Christ are said in the name of the entire holy people as well as of all present. And the visible signs used by the liturgy to signify invisible divine things have been chosen by Christ or the Church" (SC 33).

From these considerations it follows that a do-it-yourself

attitude is not acceptable in the public worship of the Church. It does damage to the Church's worship and to the faith of the people. The people of God have the right to liturgy celebrated as the Church wishes (see RS 12). The mysteries of Christ should not be celebrated as personal taste or whim may indicate. "The 'treasure' is too important and precious to risk impoverishment or compromise through forms of experimentation or practices introduced without a careful review on the part of the competent ecclesiastical authorities" (EE 51).

Creativity in Liturgical Celebrations

One may now ask whether there is any room for creativity in the liturgy. The answer is that there is, but it has to be properly understood.

First of all, it is necessary to bear in mind that the public worship of the Church is something we receive in faith through the Church. It is not something we invent. Indeed, the essentials of the sacraments are established by Christ himself. And the detailed rites, including words and actions, have been carefully worked out, guarded, and handed down by the Church through the centuries. It would, therefore, not be the proper attitude for an individual or a committee to keep thinking and planning each week how to invent a new way of celebrating Mass.

Moreover, what has priority at Mass and other liturgical acts is the worship of God. The liturgy is not a field for self-expression, free creation, and the demonstration of personal tastes. Idiosyncrasies tend to attract attention to the person rather than to the mysteries of Christ being celebrated. They can also upset, puzzle, annoy, mislead, or confuse the congregation.

Nevertheless, it is also true that the liturgical norms do allow some flexibility. With reference to the central and most important liturgical action, the Mass, for example, we can speak of three levels of flexibility. First, there are in the missal and the lectionary some alternative texts, rites, chants, readings, and blessings from which the priest celebrant can choose (see GIRM 24; RS 39). Then there are choices left to the competence of the diocesan Bishop or the Conference of Bishops, for example, the regulation of concelebration, norms regarding the distribution of Communion under both kinds, the construction and ordering of churches, translations, and some gestures (see SC 38, 40; GIRM 387, 390). Some such alternatives require *recognitio* from the Holy See. The most demanding level of variability concerns inculturation in the strict sense. It involves action by the Conference of Bishops, after conducting thorough interdisciplinary studies, and *recognitio* from the Holy See. All this has been discussed in the preceding chapter.

Redemptionis Sacramentum is therefore able to say that "ample flexibility is given for appropriate creativity aimed at allowing each celebration to be adapted to the needs of the participants, to their comprehension, their interior preparation and their gifts, according to established liturgical norms" (RS 39). The last phrase is important: "according to established liturgical norms". This paragraph of *Redemptionis Sacramentum* concludes with the crucial observation that "it should be remembered that the power of the liturgical celebrations does not consist in frequently altering the rites, but in probing more deeply the word of God and the mystery being celebrated." What the people are asking for every Sunday from their pastor is not novelty but a celebration of the sacred mysteries that nourishes faith, manifests devotion, awakens piety, leads to prayer, and incites to active charity in daily life.

Making the Mass Interesting

Many priests are concerned with making the Eucharistic celebration interesting. And they are not wrong. The Mass is not a dull carrying out of rituals. It is a vital celebration of the central mysteries of our salvation.

Care should be taken to prepare well for each celebration. The texts to be read, sung, or proclaimed should be thoroughly studied well ahead of time. The vestments and all altar fittings and furnishings should be in good taste. The people who carry out the roles of priest celebrant, altar servers, musicians, readers, and so on, should be at their best. The homily should give the people solid liturgical, theological, and spiritual nourishment. If all that is done, the Mass will not be dull.

But when all is said and done, we have to come back to the fact that the Mass is not there to entertain people. Such horizontalism would be out of place. People do not come to Mass in order to admire the preacher or the choir or the readers. The primary movement or direction of the Mass is vertical, toward God, not horizontal, toward one another. What the people need is a faith-filled celebration, a spiritual experience that draws them to God and, therefore, also to their neighbor. As a by-product, such a celebration will capture the people's interest and attention.

It is also useful to remark that repetition of faith formulae and symbols, or of familiar words and gestures, need not make a liturgical celebration uninteresting. It does matter, however, to what extent these formulae are understood; hence the importance of catechesis. In our daily lives, is it uninteresting for us to repeat our names or those of our loved ones? Do we not love our national anthem and sing it with piety? How much more should this be true of something related to our Christian identity!

Let me recall once again that liturgical celebrations allow for flexibility, provided this is done according to approved norms. *Redemptionis Sacramentum* itself exhorts the Bishop not to stifle alternative choices provided for by the liturgical norms: "The Bishop must take care not to allow the removal of that liberty foreseen by the norms of the liturgical books so that the celebration may be adapted in an intelligent manner to the church building, or to the group of the faithful who are present, or to the particular pastoral circumstances" (RS 21). It is for this reason that the Bishop does well not to be tempted to introduce unnecessary restrictions in his diocese, such as ordering that only one particular Eucharistic Prayer be used at Mass. The Bishop's authority is never firmer than when he uses it to ensure that the general norms that safeguard the tradition are observed.

In general, with respect to whether the liturgical celebration is interesting or not, the best advice is simply to celebrate it with faith and devotion and according to the approved norms, and leave the rest to God's grace and people's cooperation with it.

Formalism and Ritualism Not the Goal

From all that has been said above, it follows that an exhortation to be faithful to liturgical norms is not an invitation to formalism, ritualism, or rubricism. People are not being invited to a dry and soulless carrying out of external actions. Jesus our Savior already, quoting the prophet Isaiah, condemned those who do not internalize in their spirit the external rites they carry out:

> This people honors me with their lips,
> but their heart is far from me;

in vain do they worship me,
teaching as doctrines the precepts of men.
—Mt 15:8–9; see Is 29:13

Liturgical celebrations are not primarily the observance of norms but rather the celebration of the mysteries of Christ by the Church and in the Church, with faith and love and with respect for tradition. The observance of norms is a consequence and fruit of faith and respect. It is not the final object of worship. It is a quality of it.

For the benefit of those who are still not convinced that it is important to observe liturgical norms, may we recall what happened to Aaron's sons. In the Old Testament when Aaron's sons, Nadab and Abihu, loaded their thuribles with fire, put incense on the fire, and presented unauthorized fire before Yahweh, a flame leapt out from Yahweh's presence and swallowed them up (see Lev 10:1–5). If every priest, deacon, extraordinary minister of Holy Communion, or other member of the faithful who disregarded a liturgical norm today were to be struck down, some sanctuaries would have more than one corpse!

Liturgical norms are not arbitrary laws or regulations put together to please some historian or aesthetist or archaeologist. They are manifestations of what we believe and what we have received from tradition, from the "norm of the holy Fathers" (see SC 50; GIRM 6), from what generations of our predecessors in the faith have said, done, observed, and celebrated.

To know that we are doing, saying, hearing, and seeing what millions of Christians have done throughout the world for hundreds of years—and are doing today—should help us to enter better into a committed and prayerful participation. Moreover, by conforming our entire person to all that the liturgy represents, we undergo a transformation and become ever closer to God.

Interior prayer and sacrifice have priority. Hence the importance in liturgical celebrations of quiet preparation, silence, reflection, listening, and personal prayer. "A merely external observation of norms would obviously be contrary to the nature of the sacred liturgy, in which Christ himself wishes to gather his Church, so that together with himself she will be 'one body and one spirit'" (RS 5).

At the same time it needs to be repeated that the spirit of rejecting rules and regulations, regarded as a violation of one's autonomy, needs to be corrected. It is wrong and unreasonable to maintain an attitude of "Nobody is going to tell me what to do." This would be a false understanding of liberty. "God has not granted us in Christ an illusory liberty by which we may do what we wish, but a liberty by which we may do that which is fitting and right" (RS 7).

We should thank God that each priest and each community does not have to work out the details of how to celebrate the mysteries of Christ in the Holy Eucharist. The Church has already worked it all out for us. We have only to study and understand, love and carry out the sacred rites as directed by our Holy Mother the Church, and we shall have life, and have it in abundance, and our parishes will have liturgical peace and growth, and have them in good measure.

9

EUCHARISTIC CELEBRATION
AND MISSION

Mission of the Church

By "mission" we mean everything that Christ sent the Church to do. Aware that he himself was sent by his eternal Father, Jesus sent his Apostles and, through them, the whole Church: "As the Father sent me, so am I sending you" (Jn 20:21). They are to be his witnesses "not only in Jerusalem but throughout Judea and Samaria, and indeed to earth's remotest end" (Acts 1:8).

Mission is also called evangelization. It is not accomplished in a single act; rather it has many elements, such as silent witness to Christ, proclamation and catechesis, conversion and Baptism, establishment of local Churches, incarnation of the Gospel in cultures, meeting people of other religions, promotion of development in society, and solidarity with the needy (see REM 41–60; EN 17; DM 13).

It would therefore be an unacceptable restriction of the concept of mission to understand it as referring only to catechesis and conversion. No, mission covers the entire mandate given by Christ to his Church.

To carry out such a demanding assignment, the Church has always understood the Holy Eucharist as playing a major and irreplaceable role in preparing Christians for mission and nourishing them in it. How does this happen?

Eucharistic Celebration Sends Us on Mission

At the celebration of the Eucharistic Sacrifice we are fed at the two tables of the Word of God and of the Body and Blood of Christ.

In the first part of the Mass we receive the Word of God. The Sacred Scriptures are proclaimed. We sing psalms and canticles. Jesus speaks to us in the Gospel. In the homily, the biblical readings and other liturgical texts are explained to us and are related to the realities of our life in the world of today. If all this is done well, then we, much like the two disciples on the way to Emmaus, should find our hearts burning within us (see Lk 24:32). We should be better enlightened on the mysteries of Christ, on what God is saying to us, and on what he is sending us to do.

The second table is that of the Body and Blood of Christ. Jesus feeds us with himself. "If you do not eat the flesh of the Son of man and drink his blood, you have no life in you. . . . My flesh is real food and my blood is real drink. . . . As the living Father sent me and I draw life from the Father, so whoever eats me will also draw life from me" (Jn 6:53, 55, 57). The words of Jesus are clear, unambiguous, unmistakable. "Remain in me, as I in you" (Jn 15:4). This mutual abiding between Christ and the disciple is furthered in an exceptional way when we receive Jesus in Holy Communion. This sacrament promotes our union with Christ, increases the life of God, or grace, within us, and thus puts us in a good position to carry out our share in the mission of the Church.

Pope John Paul II called attention to this great power of

the Eucharist in preparing us for mission: "From the perpetuation of the sacrifice of the Cross and her communion with the Body and the Blood of Christ in the Eucharist, the Church draws the spiritual power needed to carry out her mission. The Eucharist thus appears as both the source and the summit of all evangelization, since its goal is the communion of mankind with Christ and in him with the Father and the Holy Spirit" (EE 22). The Pope returned to the same theme in his Apostolic Letter to prepare the Church for the Year of the Eucharist: "The encounter with Christ, constantly intensified and deepened in the Eucharist, issues in the Church and in every Christian an urgent summons to testimony and evangelization. . . . Each member of the faithful must assimilate, through personal and communal meditation, the values which the Eucharist expresses, the attitudes it inspires, the resolutions to which it gives rise" (MND 24–25).

The Holy Spirit, "the principal agent of evangelization" (EN 75), also fills us with his graces when we receive the Eucharistic Christ. The Church prays to the Father in the third Eucharistic Prayer: "Grant that we who are nourished by his Body and Blood may be filled with his Holy Spirit, and become one body, one spirit in Christ" (RM). "By the gift of his Body and Blood", said Pope John Paul II, "Christ increases within us the gift of his Spirit, already poured out in Baptism and bestowed as a 'seal' in the sacrament of Confirmation" (EE 17).

It is therefore clear that the Holy Eucharist prepares us for mission. At the end of the Mass we are sent. The directive "Ite Missa Est" really means, not "Go, the Mass is ended", but rather, "Go, you are sent now to live and share what we have received, what we have heard and what we have sung, meditated, and prayed."

Let us now take a look at four of the ways in which we can carry out this mission.

Eucharist and Proclamation

The first act of evangelization to which the Holy Eucharist sends us is proclamation. We are to share with other people the Good News that Jesus Christ is the one and only Savior of all. No matter how good the witness we give to Christ by our lives, there comes a time when we have to proclaim him in clear words. "There is no true evangelization if the name, the teaching, the life, the promises, the kingdom, and the mystery of Jesus of Nazareth, the Son of God, are not proclaimed" (EN 22).

We are to proclaim that Jesus Christ is Lord. In him alone "can be found the key, the focal point, and the goal of all human history" (GS 10). In him is the mystery of God revealed to us, and it is he who thus "fully reveals man to himself and makes his supreme calling clear" (GS 22). Jesus is the way, the truth, and the life (see Jn 14:6). To follow him is the road to salvation for all peoples, cultures, and times. The Gospel of Jesus Christ is at home among all peoples. This Gospel does not change according to majority votes or public opinion or what people are saying or doing. Jesus Christ is the same yesterday, today, and forever (see Heb 13:8).

This is the Gospel that all Christians are to proclaim, whether they be lay faithful, clerics, or consecrated men and women. Each of them has a definite role to play in the Church and in the world: in the family, in the place of work and play, in science and culture, in trade and commerce, in politics and government, and, indeed, in their entire lives. They must not drive themselves into self-made catacombs just when the world is expecting the disciples of Christ to stand up and be counted! Our Catholic faith is not a contraband good to be smuggled across the customs that is modern society. No, it is the Good News of Jesus Christ to be proclaimed and announced from the rooftops in midday sunshine (that is, with modern means of communication, especially radio, press, television, computer, Internet, video, and their derivatives).

Because of the key role of the family, allow me to dwell on its evangelizing vocation. Fed, strengthened, and sent by the Holy Eucharist, Christian families can do great things for God by evangelizing. The parents are the first educators in the faith with regard to their children. They teach their children by word and example. The children, on their part, can edify the parents with a more generous and fresh response to the Gospel message.

Families can, and should, evangelize other families. Newly married spouses can be helped by older and more experienced husbands and wives to learn to accept one another with all their virtues and weaknesses. Spouses in crisis who may be thinking of divorce can be greatly aided by loving and wise couples who give them good examples of forgiveness, large-heartedness, patience, Christian charity, and a basic acceptance of the fact that we are not yet in heaven, where everyone and everything will be found perfect. Parents who have problem children need to be evangelized by older and wiser couples who show them how to relate with difficult teenage children or with rebellious offspring. While a priest can preach on all these matters, the example and advice of experienced couples have a power of their own to help, encourage, and convince young husbands and wives to keep making the necessary effort.

Pope Paul VI summarized all this in 1975:

The family, like the Church, ought to be a place where the Gospel is transmitted and from which the Gospel radiates. In a family which is conscious of this mission, all the members evangelize and are evangelized. The parents not only communicate the Gospel to their children, but from their children they can themselves receive the same Gospel as deeply lived by them. And such a family becomes the evangelizer of many other families, and of the neighborhood of which it forms part. (EN 71; see also FC 52)

Pope Benedict XVI underlined the key role of the family in his address to Rome's Ecclesial Diocesan Convention on June 6, 2005. "Christian families constitute a crucial resource for education in the faith, for the edification of the Church as communion and for her ability to be a missionary presence in the most varied situations of life, as well as to act as a Christian leaven in the widespread culture and social structures." [1]

The October 2005 Synod of Bishops emphasized the role of the family, nourished by the Eucharist, in evangelizing its members, other families, and the larger society (see prop. 8, 15).

Evangelizing families will thus educate their children to be good citizens, will encourage their children to take part in parish programs and Catholic associations or movements, and will rejoice when God calls some of their children to the priesthood or the consecrated life. Christian solidarity shown to the poor and the needy will not be forgotten, since charity is one of the signs of an authentic Eucharistic community.

Allow me to single out for special mention the role and duty of Christian families in defending marriage and the family and promoting them in the world of today. Marriage, along with the family, is in many ways under attack in our world. It is undermined by a secularistic mentality that wants

---

[1] Benedict XVI, "Address to Rome's Ecclesial Diocesan Convention: Living the Truth That 'God Loves His People'", *L'Osservatore Romano*, weekly Eng. ed., 24 (June 15, 2005): 6.

people to live as if God did not exist. It is attacked by a materialistic and hedonistic mind-set that ignores the Maker's instructions, the divine will, regarding marriage and the family and concentrates on material enjoyment. Marriage and the family are betrayed by marital infidelity, scorned by immorality, commercialized by prostitution, banalized by pornography, ridiculed by same-sex unions, and cut in two by divorce. Saint Paul exhorts us to avoid all such evils and to behave as children of light. "Try to discover what the Lord wants of you, take no part in the futile works of darkness but, on the contrary, show them up for what they are" (Eph 5:10–11).

Christian families need to organize themselves in order better to defend marriage and the family. They will find help in approved Christian family enrichment programs in the Church. The Holy Eucharist empowers families to evangelize.

Commitment to the Earthly City

I have already mentioned in chapter 2 above that the Eucharist commits us to the improvement of life in this world. Let us go into greater detail.

The Holy Eucharist also sends us to be relevant citizens of the earthly city, to make our contribution so that this world will be a better place in which to live. The Christian has to learn to make a vital synthesis of religious duties, on the one hand, and civic duties, on the other. Not only are the two not opposed, but rather our religion manifests itself in our daily life as citizens. The Second Vatican Council warns: "The Christian who neglects his temporal duties neglects his duties toward his neighbor and even God and jeopardizes his eternal salvation" (GS 43). These are rather strong words.

It is true that our faith, with the Eucharistic celebration as its central cultic expression, prepares us for "a new heaven and a new earth" (Rev 21:1). This increases rather than lessens our commitment to making a better world, our responsibility, as citizens of the earthly city, to build a more human world, a world more in harmony with God's plan. Therefore the promotion of justice, peace, development, and harmony is very much a part of our religion. It is not something outside it. The Second Vatican Council puts it this way: "While we are warned that it profits a man nothing if he gain the whole world and lose himself, the expectation of a new earth must not weaken but rather stimulate our concern for cultivating this one. For here grows the body of a new human family, a body which even now is able to give some kind of foreshadowing of the new age" (GS 39).

For these reasons, Pope John Paul II listed this concern for the good of society as one of the areas to be attended to in the Year of the Eucharist. Our troubled world, which began the third millennium with the specter of terrorism and the tragedy of war, he said: "demands that Christians learn to experience the Eucharist as a great school of peace, forming men and women who, at various levels of responsibility in social, cultural and political life, can become promoters of dialogue and communion" (MND 27).

To make all this more concrete, here are some questions that can help us to examine our conscience on our commitment to the earthly city. What have I done to improve life for the people in my village, street, town, state, and country? In my work as teacher, doctor, nurse, taxi driver, police officer, or shoemaker, am I honest and competent so that people are happy and grateful when I have worked for them or with them? If I am a trader, do I tell the truth or, on the contrary, do I cheat people in the market? During political elections, am I honest and noble, or do I tell lies about others and regard those who do not share my political stand as enemies? Do I help in any way to rig elections and thus cheat the electorate? Is winning an election for me a question of do or die? If I am working as an employee of the government or of a company, am I dependable, or, on the contrary, do I take bribes and embezzle money? In general, do I regard my fellow citizens as brothers and sisters who are my partners in the pilgrimage that is life in this world? The Holy Eucharist sends me to be a relevant and contributing citizen in this earthly community.

Christian Solidarity with the Poor

Part of the mission that the Eucharistic celebration assigns to us is Christian solidarity with people who are in need. Saint John the Evangelist gives us the beautiful and very dramatic account of Jesus washing the feet of his Apostles. This event takes place at the critical time when the stay of our Savior in this world is approaching its end. Saint John situates the account in just the same place where the three Synoptic Gospels give their report on the institution of the Holy Eucharist at the Last Supper. Jesus teaches the Apostles to wash one another's feet. The Eucharistic overtones are unmistakable.

Saint Paul teaches the Corinthians that their participation in the Holy Eucharist is defective if they have divisions among them, if they are selfish, or if the rich are indifferent toward the poor (see 1 Cor 11:17–22; 27–34).

The Holy Eucharist commits us to love the poor and to come to their help (see CCC 1397). Saint John Chrysostom is unambiguous: "You have tasted the Blood of the Lord, yet you do not recognize your brother. . . . You dishonor this table when you do not judge worthy of sharing your food someone judged worthy to take part in this meal. . . . God freed you from all your sins and invited you here, but you have not become more merciful."[2] Jesus himself tells us that the last judgment will be based on how we have shown solidarity to the hungry, the thirsty, the stranger, the naked, the sick, and the imprisoned (see Mt 25:31–46).

Pope John Paul II said that a good criterion to use in judging the authenticity of our Eucharistic celebrations is our solidarity with such people in need. Indeed, he suggested that each diocesan or parish community undertake some such project as part of its initiative in the Year of the Eucharist (see MND 28).

When Catholics show solidarity with the needy, they are not just social workers. They are witnesses of Christ. They are living out their Eucharistic celebration.

Meeting People of Other Religions

The Holy Eucharist sends us to be witnesses of Christ among all people, whether they believe in Christ or not. The Church sees herself as "a kind of sacrament or sign of intimate union with God and of the unity of all mankind" (LG 1).

Many levels of contact with people of other religions can be observed. There is first that of good will and mutual respect. Next comes mutual listening, which can bring with it better understanding of the religious positions of one another. Where the partners in dialogue persevere, collaboration in the promotion of social works can follow, to the benefit of society. When mutual trust grows, and if the collaborators are sufficiently prepared theologically, they can enter into an exchange at the theological level.

[2] Saint John Chrysostom, *Hom. in 1 Cor.* 27, 4 (PG 61, 229–30).

The Christian, in his contact with people of other religions, cannot, avoid the fact that these people have the right to hear the Good News of Jesus Christ and to be introduced into faith in him. A necessary condition is that they freely welcome such proclamation. The right to religious freedom of which the 1948 United Nations Universal Declaration of Human Rights speaks in paragraph 18 includes the right to change one's religion. The Second Vatican Council notes that people are "bound by a moral obligation to seek the truth, especially religious truth. They are also bound to adhere to the truth, once it is known, and to order their whole lives in accord with the demands of truth" (DH 2). Only thus can every individual be properly answerable to God for the use of freedom.

It follows, therefore, that no individual or government has the right to forbid conversion to Christianity or to Catholicism. It is also a necessary consequence that Christians have the obligation to share the Gospel of Jesus Christ with people of other religions who freely want to hear it. Such a sharing is not proselytism. It is evangelization. Pope Paul VI insisted in clear terms that interreligious dialogue or respect does not make proclamation unnecessary: "Neither respect and esteem for these religions nor the complexity of the questions raised is an invitation to the Church to withhold from these non-Christians the proclamation of Jesus Christ. On the contrary, the Church holds that these multitudes have the right to know the riches of the mystery of Christ" (EN 53; see also DP 82).

When, therefore, we reflect that the Holy Eucharist sends us to meet our fellow men, we are to see ourselves as sent to share with them the best treasures we have, as respect for the human person and prudence may advise in each concrete context.

Our contacts with other Christians who are not in union with the Catholic Church is not interreligious dialogue but ecumenism. We must pray and work for the reunion of Christians. And we should be of help to individuals who want to regain full communion with the Catholic Church. Indeed, the Eucharistic celebration does make serious demands on us.

10

WORSHIP OF THE HOLY EUCHARIST
OUTSIDE MASS

After Mass, Jesus continues to be present in the Eucharistic mystery. "The Eucharistic presence of Christ", says the *Catechism of the Catholic Church*, "begins at the moment of the consecration and endures as long as the Eucharistic species subsist" (CCC 1377). This is the foundation of reverence to the Holy Eucharist outside Mass. "The Catholic Church has always offered and still offers to the sacrament of the Eucharist the cult of adoration, not only during Mass, but also outside of it, reserving the consecrated hosts with the utmost care, exposing them to the solemn veneration of the faithful, and carrying them in procession" (MF 56; see also CCC 1378).

The Most Blessed Sacrament is kept in the tabernacle for several reasons. The first is so that the Eucharist can be brought to the sick and the old who cannot come to Mass. Then, in the tabernacle Jesus awaits our visits of faith, adoration, praise, love, and thanksgiving. Also, we visit him to ask pardon for our sins and the sins of others, to make reparation, and to make other requests (cf. DC 31).

This explains why veneration of the Eucharistic mystery has flowered in such forms as personal prayer before the

Blessed Sacrament, hours of adoration, periods of Eucharistic exposition (short, prolonged, and annual Forty Hours), Eucharistic Benediction, Eucharistic processions, and Eucharistic congresses. The Solemnity of the Body and Blood of Christ is known throughout the Latin Church because of its extremely beautiful liturgical texts and the solemn Eucharistic procession that follows Mass. Pope John Paul II every year led the traditional Eucharistic procession from the Basilica of Saint John Lateran to that of Saint Mary Major, a tradition continued by Pope Benedict XVI.

It would be a mistake to imagine that the Church since the Second Vatican Council has laid less stress on these manifestations of faith. The contrary is the case. For proof of this, just consider the Encyclical Letters, Apostolic Letters, and Instructions listed in the first chapter of this book.

The tabernacle in which the Most Blessed Sacrament is reserved is traditionally given special attention by the Church. Paragraphs 314 to 316 of the introductory instructions of the *Roman Missal* of 2002 give it a prominent place. The tabernacle should be in a part of the church that is really noble, distinguished, conspicuous, well decorated, and suitable for prayer (see October 2005 Synod, prop. 28). It should be placed either in the sanctuary, apart from the altar of celebration in the most suitable form and place, or even in a chapel suitable for adoration and the personal prayer of the faithful and which is integrally connected with the church and is conspicuous to the faithful. A sanctuary lamp, fed by oil or wax, should burn near the tabernacle to indicate that Jesus is present. Compare these official instructions to what is sometimes the case in some churches, especially those restructured by some ill-informed reformers. In some such churches, one cannot tell where the tabernacle is. Then one can in truth lament: "They have taken my Lord away and I do not know where they have put him" (Jn 20:13).

The Congregation for the Clergy, in its Instruction of August 4, 2002, advises priests:

> The Blessed Sacrament is to be lovingly reserved in a tabernacle "which is the spiritual heart of every religious and parochial community". Without the cult of the Eucharist, as with a beating heart, a parish becomes arid. If you wish the faithful to pray willingly and piously—as Pius XII reminded the clergy of Rome—set an example for them by praying in your churches before them. A priest on his knees before the tabernacle, with a proper disposition and in deep recollection, is a model of edification for the people, a reminder of, and an invitation to, prayerful emulation. (PPL 21)

People want to venerate our Eucharistic Lord on bended knee. To facilitate this, there should be kneelers in front of the Blessed Sacrament. I have seen specially built twenty-four-hour Eucharistic adoration chapels where some people freely prostrate themselves when they are so inclined, without any attention to what other people might think of them. If you really believe that Jesus is there, God and Man, is it not logical to prostrate yourself?

When Pope Benedict XVI and the Synod Fathers met at the XI Ordinary Assembly of the Synod of Bishops in October 2005, they gave special importance to Eucharistic adoration (see prop. 6). Recognizing the many fruits of this practice in the lives of the people of God all around the world, the Synod recalled how this form of prayer was frequently recommended by the Servant of God Pope John Paul II. The Synod strongly recommended that this prayer be kept up and promoted according to the traditions of both the Latin Church and the Oriental Churches. Eucharistic adoration, the Synod said, originates from the Eucharistic celebration of the Mass, which is the greatest act of adoration performed by the Church. Eucharistic adoration enables the faithful to participate more fully, consciously, actively, and fruitfully in the Sacrifice of Christ according to the desires of the Second Vatican Council. It also leads back to the Mass.

When lived in this way, noted the Synod, Eucharistic adoration sustains the faithful in their Christian love and service toward others. It also promotes greater holiness both in individuals and in the Christian community. For this reason, the reflowering of Eucharistic adoration, evident also among young people, should be seen as a promising characteristic of many communities. To favor this, the Synod wanted church buildings where the Most Blessed Sacrament is reserved to be left open as far as possible, to facilitate people's opportunity for Eucharistic adoration.

The Synod went farther and urged adequate pastoral measures to help communities, associations, and movements to appreciate the importance of such adoration and to cultivate the consequent attitude of wondering contemplation in front of the great gift of the Real Presence of Christ. It encouraged Eucharistic adoration for those preparing for First Communion. And it praised institutes of the consecrated life and associations of Christ's faithful that promote Eucharistic adoration in various ways. This Eucharistic devotion should become more and more biblical, liturgical, and missionary.

The Synod did not just speak and write on Eucharistic adoration. It went into action. Each day Synod participants were seen adoring Jesus exposed in the monstrance in the chapel next to the Synod hall one hour before both the morning and the evening sessions. Moreover, in the evening of October 17, 2005, the Holy Father and all the Synod participants adored our Eucharistic Lord for an hour in Saint Peter's Basilica. A large number of lay faithful, priests, and consecrated people took part in that beautiful combination of Eucharistic hymns, appropriate Bible readings, intercessory prayers, and prolonged periods of personal prayer. At the end, Jesus exposed in the monstrance gave the assembly his blessing. The entire act was more eloquent than all the propositions of the Synod and its concluding *Message* put together!

It is a beautiful practice for people who are near a church or chapel where the august Sacrament is reserved to pay visits to our Lord, short or long as the case may be. There is also the praiseworthy habit of making the Sign of the Cross or bowing when one drives past such a sacred place.

Indeed, we could continue recounting many more ways in which the faith of Catholics in the Holy Eucharist can manifest itself in acts of reverence.

11

THE CENTRALITY OF
THE EUCHARISTIC CELEBRATION IN
THE LIFE AND WORSHIP OF THE CHURCH

The preceding reflections lead us to the unfailing conclusion that the Eucharistic celebration is central to the life and worship of the Church.

Eucharistic Sacrifice: Summit and Center of Liturgical Life

Nothing that the Church does in her liturgical worship is as solemn and elevated as the sacramental re-presentation of the paschal mystery of Christ the Lord. The only liturgical act as great as the Mass is, well, another Mass!

As quoted earlier, the Second Vatican Council calls the Eucharistic Sacrifice "the fount and apex of the whole Christian life" (LG 11). The liturgy as a whole "is the summit toward which the activity of the Church is directed; at the same time it is the fountain from which all her power flows. ... From the liturgy, therefore, and especially from the Eucharist, as from a fountain, grace is channeled into us; and the sanctification of people in Christ and the glorification of God, to which all other activities of the Church are directed as toward their goal, are most powerfully achieved" (SC 10).

"The other sacraments, and indeed all ecclesiastical ministries and works of the apostolate, are bound up with the Eucharist and are oriented toward it. For in the blessed Eucharist is contained the whole spiritual good of the Church, namely, Christ himself, our Pasch" (PO 5).

The sacraments of Baptism, Confirmation, Holy Orders, and Matrimony are celebrated within the Mass, as can be the Anointing of the Sick. Penance prepares people to participate in the Holy Eucharist. Thus the entire sacramental system is oriented toward the Holy Eucharist.

Many sacramentals, such as profession of religious brothers and sisters, the dedication of a church or altar, and the blessing of chalices and patens, are also located within the Eucharistic Sacrifice.

The Liturgy of the Hours, that is, the prayers of the Church for the different hours of the day, are also oriented toward the Eucharist, and there is provision for some of them to be celebrated within the Mass.

Considering that "the Church draws her life from Christ in the Eucharist; by him she is fed and by him she is enlightened" (EE 6), it follows that the Eucharist "stands at the center of the Church's life" (EE 3). Pope Paul VI had earlier made an observation in the same sense: "If the sacred liturgy holds first place in the life of the Church, then the Eucharistic Mystery stands at the heart and center of the liturgy, since it is the font of life that cleanses us and strengthens us" (MF 2). Pope Benedict XVI in his first message to the Cardinals, delivered, after Mass, in the Sistine Chapel on April 20, 2005, called the Eucharist "the heart of Christian life and the source of the Church's evangelizing mission". He continued: "The Eucharist makes constantly present the Risen Christ who continues to give himself to us, calling us to participate in the banquet of his Body and his Blood. From full communion with him flows every other element of the Church's life: first of all, communion among all the faithful, the commitment to proclaiming and witnessing to the Gospel, the ardour of love for all, especially the poorest and lowliest." [1]

The Sunday Eucharist

The Church of the Roman Rite celebrates the Holy Eucharist every day, except on Good Friday and Holy Saturday. But from the earliest centuries the Sunday Eucharist has had great importance. The Church in a diocese manifests herself in a special way when the diocesan Bishop celebrates the Eucharistic Sacrifice in his cathedral church, with the concelebration of his priests, the assistance of deacons, and the active participation of all the people of God (see SC 41). Every Eucharistic celebration in the diocese, especially the parish Mass, is related to the Bishop, even when he does not preside (see LG 26; RS 20).

The Sunday Eucharist has great importance because it is celebrated on the day when Christ conquered death and gave us a share in his immortal life. The mystery of the Church is concretely made present (see DD 34). The Acts of the Apostles tells us that the early Christian community "remained faithful to the teaching of the Apostles, to the brotherhood, to the breaking of bread and to the prayers" (Acts 2:42). When some Christians in later centuries became half-hearted or negligent in coming to Sunday Eucharist, the Church increasingly made explicit the duty to participate at Sunday Mass, as in the Council of Elvira in 300 and finally in the Code of Canon Law in 1917, when this tradition became universal law.

---

[1] Benedict XVI, Message "Striving to Be the 'Servus servorum Dei'", no. 4, *L'Osservatore Romano*, weekly Eng. ed., 17 (April 27, 2005): 4.

There is therefore a grave obligation to participate at the Eucharistic celebration on Sundays and major solemnities. The Mass is the heart of Sunday. This explains why priests and Bishops take great pains to provide the Christian communities with the Sunday Eucharist. It is also the reason why many devoted people are willing to travel miles in order to have Sunday Mass. Every convinced Catholic should be able to say with the Martyrs of Abitene in North Africa during the Diocletian persecution (304–305): "We cannot live without the Lord's Supper" (Sunday Mass) (quoted in DD 46).

The Parish: A Eucharistic Community

A parish is a definite community of the Christian faithful established on a stable basis within a particular Church or diocese. The Bishop entrusts the pastoral care of the parish to a pastor. A parish is a community of worship; it teaches Christian doctrine; it practices charity in good works and brotherly love.

As a community of worship, the parish initiates people into the Christian fold by incorporation into the Church at Baptism and brings them into participation in the liturgical life of the Church. The high point of this parish liturgical celebration is the Sunday Eucharist. The Second Vatican Council stresses this: "Efforts also must be made to encourage a sense of community within the parish, above all in the common celebration of the Sunday Mass" (SC 42; see also CCC 2179). The parish Sunday Eucharist is seen by the Church as "the celebration which brings together the entire parish community, with the participation of different groups, movements, and associations" (MND 23; see also DD 35–36; October 2005 Synod, prop. 30, 32; EM 26; RS 114).

The parish also fulfills a teaching role. It brings the Word of God to the people and teaches them Christian doctrine. This is another great service of the Sunday Mass. For most Catholics, it is the one occasion in the week where they can be fed on the truths of the faith. The Scripture readings, the psalms, and the homily build up the faith. Then together as a community, the people sing or recite the Symbol of the Faith, the Creed, the words of which are hallowed by almost two millennia of liturgical profession.

The parish is, thirdly, a community of charity, of service, and of Christian solidarity with the needy, as we shall discuss farther down.

The parish should therefore be seen as a Eucharistic community, especially when it gathers at Sunday Mass. "No Christian community can be built up unless it has its basis and center in the celebration of the most Holy Eucharist. Here, therefore, all education in the spirit of community must originate" (PO 6; see also EE 32–33).

The Religious Institute or Monastery: A Eucharistic Community

The community formed by the members of an institute of consecrated life, by a religious congregation, or by a monastery has the center of its daily life in the Eucharistic Sacrifice. The celebration of daily Mass is the chief event in such a religious house, the main activity of the day, the center of the daily life and work of the monks or nuns, brothers or sisters. Their celebration of the Liturgy of the Hours, the work of God, is centered on the Mass. It prepares them for it and radiates from it.

In such religious houses it is best to choose an hour for Mass when almost all the members will be present, considering their various assignments. All things being equal, a morning hour when people are fresher and less distracted is preferable to midday or evening, when people tend to be tired. I admit that sometimes this is not an easy decision.

In the location of a house for consecrated people who have no priest members, consideration should be given to the availability of a priest for daily Mass. It would be a major lack if a religious community could not have Mass except on Sunday. Here tribute is due to those priest chaplains who make considerable sacrifice in time and travel in order to see that a community of consecrated people has regular daily Mass.

Religious houses will also appreciate the spiritual beauty of community hours of Eucharistic adoration in addition to visits to our Eucharistic Lord by individuals. Since a community of consecrated people is one called and gathered together by the love of Christ and held together by his grace, what better place is there for the members to return their love to Jesus than before the tabernacle?

The Holy Eucharist in My Day, My Week

Here every one of us can put to himself a personal question: What place has the Holy Eucharist in my life?

If I am able to participate at Mass every day, do I make a sincere effort to do so? Do I see my daily Mass as the supreme moment in my day to adore God, to acknowledge his greatness, to offer him praise and thanks, and to propitiate him for my sins and those of others? Do I see the Eucharistic Sacrifice as a golden opportunity to offer Christ to God the Father and to learn to offer myself through Christ? Is daily Mass appreciated by me as a liturgically rich event in which I put before God my whole day, with its joys and sorrows, projects, achievements, and disappointments?

Do I look forward to a meeting with Jesus in Holy Communion? He has invited us to come to him: "Remain in me, as I in you . . . for cut off from me you can do nothing" (Jn 15:4–5). Indeed, he warns us: "If you do not eat the flesh of the Son of man and drink his blood, you have no life in you" (Jn 6:53). And he reassures us: "Whoever eats my flesh and drinks my blood lives in me and I live in that person" (Jn 6:56). Is it not a wonderful thing that we can receive Jesus each day of our earthly pilgrimage?

What is Sunday Mass for me? Do I see it as a privileged participation in this tribute of worship offered to God by the Christian community of which I am part? Do I see it as a profession of faith in the one, holy, Catholic, and apostolic Church? Do I appreciate the opportunity it affords to give powerful Christian witness, to encourage one another in the practice of the faith, and to sing joyfully together with others before the Lord? The exhortation of Saint John Chrysostom is remarkable: "You cannot pray at home as at church, where there is a great multitude, where exclamations are cried out to God as from one great heart, and where there is something more: the union of minds, the accord of souls, the bond of charity, the prayers of the priests." [2]

Learning to Offer Ourselves

The Eucharistic Sacrifice is central in the lives of Christians who want to offer themselves to God in many senses of the word "offer".

The Mass is the offering of himself that Jesus Christ our Savior makes to his Eternal Father. He is the Victim who alone is an adequate offering to God's majesty.

Jesus associates the Church with himself in this Eucharistic

---

[2] Saint John Chrysostom, *De incomprehensibili* 3, 6 (PG 48, 725).

offering. While only the ordained priest consecrates bread and wine into the Body and Blood of Christ, all the baptized in the congregation offer Christ to the Father with and through the priest. They also learn to offer themselves through Christ, with Christ, and in Christ. So the Second Vatican Council says: "Taking part in the Eucharistic Sacrifice, which is the fount and apex of the whole Christian life, they offer the divine Victim to God, and offer themselves along with it" (LG 11).

Shall we get down to some details? Instead of lamenting our problems, it is in the Mass that we offer to God our pains and aches, our sickness, our old age, our family difficulties, situations of suffering as a result of other people's action, political headaches, and the lack of security or peace in society.

We also offer to God our plans and hopes, our studies and future prospects, our fears, our professional undertakings, our Church associations and activities, and our dreams of making this world a better place for all.

The Mass is also the moment of celebration in which to offer God our joys, our good health, our family unity, our success in our studies or profession, our circle of friends, and the quiet joy of seeing our projects bloom.

Along with the bread and wine at the offertory at Mass, we bring to God our entire selves. We beg him through Christ, with Christ, and in Christ to make of us an offering acceptable in his sight. When viewed and lived in that way, the Mass becomes more and more central in our Christian life.

Holy Eucharist at the Milestones in Personal and Community Life

Both in our personal and in our community life, the Holy Eucharist is there to be celebrated at every milestone.

The sacraments mark the major milestones in our share in the redemption worked for us by Christ. We therefore celebrate the Holy Eucharist at our reception of Baptism, Confirmation, Holy Orders, and Matrimony.

It is usual for Catholics to request the priest to offer Holy Mass for them at anniversaries and especially jubilees of such events as birth, wedding, priestly ordination, or religious profession.

Thanksgiving has as its highest expression the Eucharistic Sacrifice. When people want to thank God for the arrival of a new baby in the family, recovery from sickness, escape from danger, success in professional life, university graduation, or simply retirement from public service, they cannot think of any celebration greater than a Mass. And they are right.

Communities also arrange to have the Eucharistic celebration to mark major events. Examples are town or state anniversaries, national holidays, such as Independence Day, Thanksgiving Day, and the annual day to remember the fallen in war. Moreover, times of danger and suffering for a community call for special Masses, as in time of war, for justice and peace, and when natural disasters like earthquakes, drought, and epidemics threaten a people. The missal has a Votive Mass for many such occasions.

Seen in this way, the Holy Eucharist rightly occupies a central place in the life of a Christian or of a Christian community.

Holy Eucharist at the Sunset of Our Earthly Pilgrimage

There comes a time when indications begin increasingly to show that the end of our earthly life is not far away. Strength begins to fail. The bones start to ache. Movement slows down each day. One sickness or another is detected. In short, the evening, the twilight, the sunset of our earthly pilgrimage is beginning to unfold.

As all through life starting from infancy, so also in old age the Holy Eucharist is central to our Christian life. Jesus accompanies us with this sacrifice and sacrament. The Church sets great value on the apostolate of the hospital chaplains who celebrate Mass for the sick in hospitals or homes for the elderly and bring them Holy Communion. The sick or the old in their homes are also brought the comforting visit of their Eucharistic Lord.

When death is near, the Holy Eucharist is administered to the dying as *Viaticum*, to strengthen the dying and accompany him on the journey to eternity. Saint Ignatius of Antioch calls the Holy Eucharist the "medicine of immortality".[3]

When a Christian has died, the most important thing we can do for that person is to offer the Sacrifice of the Mass. This is also the center of a Christian funeral celebration. And after the funeral, we continue to offer the Eucharistic Sacrifice for our dear ones so that if they are in purgatory they may soon be admitted into the light and peace of Christ (see CCC 1371).

---

[3] Saint Ignatius of Antioch, *Epistula ad Ephesios* 20, 2 (SCh 10, 76), quoted in CCC 1331.

12

THE IMPORTANCE OF
LITURGICAL FORMATION

If all the people of God are to benefit as much as possible from their participation in the Eucharistic celebration, then proper liturgical formation is necessary for all. And such formation is not acquired once and for all. It is to go on throughout our lives.

The Church Urges Such Formation

A major challenge facing the Church in every age is to see that every Christian receive adequate and ongoing liturgical formation, according to each person's vocation and mission. The Second Vatican Council places priority on the liturgical preparation of the clergy, since the priest is a key figure in most liturgical celebrations. "It is vitally necessary", it insists, "that attention be directed, above all, to the liturgical instruction of the clergy" (SC 14). The Council goes on to speak of the choice of good liturgy professors for seminaries, religious houses of study, and theological faculties, of the teaching of the liturgy, of a liturgical spirituality, and of ongoing liturgical formation for priests already serving in the ministry (SC 15–18).

The Council also emphasizes the importance of the liturgical formation of the lay faithful if their hoped-for active participation in the sacred liturgy, internally and externally, is to be properly promoted (SC 19).

This challenge of liturgical information and formation for all members of the Church needs to be given priority attention. The liturgical books are to be taken in hand, studied, understood, and faithfully followed. The Holy Father Pope John Paul II drew attention to this in his Apostolic Letter of December 4, 2003, to commemorate forty years of *Sacrosanctum Concilium*. He said: "The Council's renewal of the liturgy was expressed most clearly in the publication of liturgical books. After a preliminary period in which the renewed texts were gradually incorporated into the liturgical celebrations, a deeper experience of their riches and potential has become necessary" (SS 7).[1] The recent Instruction of the Congregation for Divine Worship and the Discipline of the Sacraments notes that liturgical abuses "are often based on ignorance, in that they involve a rejection of those elements whose deeper meaning is not understood and whose antiquity is not recognized" (RS 9).

Nothing, therefore, can take the place of adequate and ongoing liturgical formation.

Scriptural Formation

Good liturgical formation presupposes adequate scriptural grounding. "Sacred Scripture is of paramount importance in the celebration of the liturgy. For it is from Scripture that lessons are read and explained in the homily, and psalms are sung; the prayers, collects, and liturgical songs are scriptural

---

[1] In: Congregazione per il Culto Divino e la Disciplina dei Sacramenti, *Spiritus et Sponsa* (2004), p. 38.

in their inspiration, and it is from Scripture that actions and signs derive their meaning" (SC 24).

In the Eucharistic celebration, Jesus feeds us with his Word and his Sacrament. The assertion of the Second Vatican Council is striking and powerful: "The Church has always venerated the divine Scriptures just as she venerates the Body of the Lord, since from the table of both the Word of God and of the Body of Christ she unceasingly receives and offers to the faithful the bread of life, especially in the sacred liturgy" (DV 21; see also SC 24).

Without knowledge of Holy Scripture, the liturgy will not be understood. Just think of the Old Testament persons who were symbols, like Abraham, Moses, Aaron, Isaac, and the Prophets, and events, things, and actions such as the paschal lamb, passover, covenant, manna, and the promised land. And how can the riches of the liturgy be approached fruitfully without knowledge of the teachings of Christ himself and of his Apostles? Therefore the Council rightly observes that "if the restoration, progress and adaptation of the sacred liturgy are to be achieved, it is necessary to promote the warm and living love for Scripture to which the venerable tradition of both Eastern and Western rites gives testimony" (SC 24). "Ignorance of the Scriptures", Saint Jerome tells us, "is ignorance of Christ." [2]

The Church therefore has offered to the people of God a more abundant and better selected body of biblical readings in the Eucharistic celebration (see SC 35). The lectionary of today is much richer than what we had before the Second Vatican Council (see SC 51). The greater care given to biblical translations for liturgical use by the Bishops' Conferences and the Congregation for Divine Worship and the

---

[2] Saint Jerome, *Commentariorum in Isaiah*, prol. (PL 24, 17B).

Discipline of Sacraments has helped. And in addition to beautifully bound lectionaries and Gospel Books carried in solemn procession, there are also parish weekly bulletins, which help people to follow the readings and to meditate on them privately.

The Word of God proclaimed in the Mass, venerated, listened to attentively, and acclaimed is able to nourish faith, to reawaken it where necessary, and to give it where needed. It "is something alive and active: it cuts more incisively than any two-edged sword" (Heb 4:12).

This proclaimed and received Word of God is transformed into prayer and song. Many liturgical prayers and hymns are deeply scriptural. Moreover, the homily draws from the fresh and living water of the Word of God to announce the wonderful things of God, to explain, apply, and prolong the reception of the Word. The homily focuses the searching light of the Word of God on the details of life on earth today, so that the people of God may see better how to live what they have celebrated (see SC 52).

Every diocese, parish, religious house, or monastery can ask itself what programs of ongoing liturgical formation it has developed for its members.

13

AT THE SCHOOL OF MARY

As we come near the end of these reflections, we cannot do better than go to the school of the Most Blessed Virgin Mary to ask her to guide us and help us know how best to take part in the Eucharistic Sacrifice.

The Eucharist is a mystery of faith that altogether surpasses our understanding and calls us to total faith and trust in the words of Jesus. Mary is our model in total faith. She who said to the servants at the Cana wedding: "Do whatever he tells you" (Jn 2:5), also tells us at Mass to trust entirely in the words of her Son, who says: "This is my Body. . . . This is my Blood." If Jesus was able to change water into wine, he can also turn bread and wine into his Body and Blood and through this mystery bestow on believers the living memorial of his paschal mystery.

"There is a profound analogy", said Pope John Paul II, "between the *Fiat* which Mary said in reply to the angel, and the *Amen* which every believer says when receiving the Body of the Lord" (EE 55).

The Virgin Mary, who contemplated the face of the new-born Christ in rapture and cradled him in her arms, is a model of the love that should inspire us every time we receive Jesus in Holy Communion.

At the Presentation of the Child Jesus in the temple, Simeon prophesied that this child would be a "sign of contradiction" and that a sword would pierce Mary's own heart (see Lk 2:34–35). From that foreshadowing we can think of Mary as in a daily offering of an anticipated Eucharist until she stood at the foot of the Cross on Calvary, offered her Son, and suffered with him. She was teaching us how to offer Christ to God the Father and also offer ourselves with Christ, through Christ, and in Christ.

Whenever after Easter the Blessed Virgin participated at the Eucharist celebrated by Peter, John, James, or the other Apostles and heard the words "This is my Body which is given for you" (Lk 22:19), we can imagine what she must have felt. Receiving the Holy Eucharist, she welcomed once more that heart which had beat in unison with hers for months, and she relived what she had experienced at the foot of the Cross. Mary teaches us to approach the Eucharistic Sacrifice as the sacramental re-presentation of the Sacrifice of Calvary and to receive Jesus with growing and loving faith and dedication.

At the Sacrifice of Calvary, Jesus entrusted his beloved Mother to John and John to his beloved Mother. When we commemorate Christ's death in the Eucharistic celebration, we in a way also receive Mary as entrusted to us, and we feel committed to be conformed to Christ by putting ourselves at the school of his Mother. "If the Church and the Eucharist are inseparably united, the same ought to be said of Mary and the Eucharist. This is one reason why, since ancient times, the commemoration of Mary has always been part of the Eucharistic celebrations of the Churches of East and West" (EE 57).

The Virgin of Nazareth received the message from the Archangel Gabriel, conceived Jesus the Son of God made man, and went with haste to visit Elizabeth. She brought

Jesus, who sanctified John the Baptist in the womb. In an analogous way, when we have been nourished at the two tables of the Word of God and of the Body and Blood of Christ at Mass, we are sent on mission. We must go with haste to evangelize, to proclaim Christ, to witness to him, to show Christian solidarity to the needy, to make this world a better place in which to live, in short, to set the whole world on fire with the love of Christ, to borrow the expression of Saint Catherine of Siena.[1]

Mary during her visit to Zechariah, Elizabeth, and John the Baptist not yet born sang God's praises in the *Magnificat*. At the Eucharistic celebration, the Church praises, thanks, and magnifies God for the wonderful work of creation, redemption, and sanctification. Through Christ our Savior, God has called us out of darkness into his wonderful light (see 1 Pet 2:9). At Mass, the Church celebrates the paschal mystery and looks forward to the new heavens and the new earth (see Rev 21:1), when Christ will come again in glory. The Church makes her own that spirituality of the Virgin Mary which we see in the *Magnificat*.

As we take part in the Eucharistic celebration, daily if possible, let us request that our Blessed Mother, "a woman of the Eucharist in her whole life" (EE 53), obtain for us the graces of continued growth in Eucharistic faith, hope, and love and in the authentic and dynamic living each day of what we have received, heard, meditated, sung, and prayed during the Eucharistic celebration.

---

[1] Saint Catherine of Siena: see Letter 368.

ABBREVIATIONS

AG   Vatican II, Decree on the Church's Missionary Activity, *Ad Gentes Divinitus*, December 7, 1965

CCC   *Catechism of the Catholic Church*, 2nd ed., Rome: Libreria Editrice Vaticana, 1997

CD   Paul VI, Decree *Christus Dominus*, October 28, 1965

CIC   *Code of Canon Law*

DC   John Paul II, Letter *Dominicae Cenae*, February 24, 1980

DD   John Paul II, Apostolic Letter *Dies Domini*, July 5, 1998

DH   Vatican II, Declaration on Religious Liberty, *Dignitatis Humanae*, December 7, 1965

DM   Secretariat for Non-Christians, *The Attitude of the Church toward the Followers of Other Religions: Reflections and Orientations on Dialogue and Mission*, May 10, 1984

DP   Pontifical Council for Inter-religious Dialogue, *Dialogue and Proclamation*, May 19, 1991

DPMB Congregation for Bishops, *Directory on the Pastoral Ministry of Bishops*, February 22, 1973

DS   Denzinger-Schönmetzer, *Enchiridion Symbolorum Definitionum et Declarationum de Rebus Fidei et Morum*

DV   Vatican II, Dogmatic Constitution on Divine Revelation, *Dei Verbum*, November 18, 1965

EA   John Paul II, Post-synodal Apostolic Exhortation *Ecclesia in Africa*, September 14, 1995

EE   John Paul II, Encyclical Letter *Ecclesia de Eucharistia*, April 17, 2003

EM   Sacred Congregation of Rites, Instruction *Eucharisticum Mysterium*, May 25, 1967

EN   Paul VI, Apostolic Exhortation *Evangelii Nuntiandi*, December 8, 1975

FC   John Paul II, Apostolic Exhortation *Familiaris Consortio*, November 22, 1981

GIRM *General Instruction of the Roman Missal*, 2002

GS   Vatican II, Pastoral Constitution on the Church in the Modern World, *Gaudium et Spes*, December 7, 1965

LA   Congregation for Divine Worship and the Discipline of the Sacraments, Instruction *Liturgiam Authenticam*, March 28, 2001

LG   Vatican II, Dogmatic Constitution on the Church, *Lumen Gentium*, November 21, 1964

MF   Paul VI, Encyclical Letter *Mysterium Fidei*, September 3, 1965

MND   John Paul II, Apostolic Letter *Mane Nobiscum Domine*, October 7, 2004

OE   Vatican II, Decree on the Catholic Eastern Churches, *Orientalium Ecclesiarum*, November 21, 1964

PO   Vatican II, Decree on the Ministry and Life of Priests, *Presbyterorum Ordinis*, December 7, 1965

PPL   Congregation for the Clergy, Instruction *The Priest: Pastor and Leader of the Parish Community*, August 4, 2002

REM   John Paul II, Encyclical Letter *Redemptoris Missio*, December 7, 1990

RM   *Roman Missal*, third typical edition, 2002

RS   Congregation for Divine Worship and the Discipline of the Sacraments, Instruction *Redemptionis Sacramentum*, March 25, 2004

SA   John Paul II, Encylical Letter *Slavorum Apostoli*, June 2, 1985

SC   Vatican II, The Constitution on the Sacred Liturgy, *Sacrosanctum Concilium*, December 4, 1963

SS   John Paul II, Apostolic Letter *Spiritus et Sponsa*, December 4, 2003

ST   Saint Thomas Aquinas, *Summa Theologiae*

VL   Congregation for Divine Worship and the Discipline of the Sacraments, Instruction *Varietates Legitimae*, January 25, 1994

VQA   John Paul II, Apostolic Letter *Vicesimus Quintus Annus*, December 4, 1988